Campus Visits
& College
Interviews

Campus Visits & College Interviews

A Complete Guide for College-Bound Students and Their Families

Third Edition

Zola Dincin Schneider and
Norman G. Schneider

The College Board
New York

The College Board is a mission driven not-for-profit organization that connects students to college success and opportunity. Founded in 1900, the College Board was created to expand access to higher education. Today, the membership association is made up of over 6,000 of the world's leading educational institutions and is dedicated to promoting excellence and equity in education. Each year, the College Board helps more than seven million students prepare for a successful transition to college through programs and services in college readiness and college success — including the SAT® and the Advanced Placement Program®. The organization also serves the education community through research and advocacy on behalf of students, educators and schools.

For further information, visit www.collegeboard.org.

Copies of this book are available from your local bookseller or may be ordered from College Board Publications, 45 Columbus Avenue, New York, NY 10023-6992. The price is $14.99.

Editorial inquiries concerning this book should be directed to The College Board, 45 Columbus Avenue, New York, NY 10023-6992.

Grateful acknowledgment is made to James Montague for permission to reproduce his list of "What Colleges Look At" on page 20.

ISBN: 978-0-87447-988-1

Printed in the United States of America.
Distributed by Macmillan.

In loving memory of my parents
Renee and Herman Dincin
and
To a new generation of family
Ben, David, Jacob, Max, Paul, Rafael and Rosie

Contents

PART 1 – THE CAMPUS VISIT

CHAPTER 1 — DECIDING TO VISIT 3

CHAPTER 2 — SELECTING COLLEGES TO VISIT 15

CHAPTER 3 — MAKING PLANS 25

PART 2 — THE INTERVIEW

Acknowledgments

Acknowledgments to the Third Edition

I am so happy that Norman Schneider has joined with me on this new edition. It is a great pleasure to share all the adventures of writing with him, but beyond that, this third edition would not have been possible without his well-honed abilities to investigate and resolve the college information explosion on the Web. Together we have edited and revised the original book, and we have written several additional chapters for this edition to bring the whole new story to college-bound students and their families.

I continually learn from all my students, but for this third edition I especially want to thank Sasha Berger, Seth Butler, Sarah Lipkowitz, Theo Salem-Mackall, David Schneider and Rafael Schneider for sharing with me their insights into the current youth scene.

I am grateful for the chats and longer discussions I've had with parents who have gone through the college admission process with their children. I have gleaned much from Joan Rabinor, Andrea Nolin, Marcy Berger and Eileen Coen about particular aspects of their college visits. In addition, Gail Forman has been of great help in discussing the editorial content of new material, Arnold and Sandy Leibowitz for telling their college stories, Judy Fardig for her encounters with the social media and Robin Hayutin for relating her alumna interview experiences.

My special thanks go to my colleagues and friends at ACCESS, IECA and NACAC who, through the years, have shared their knowledge and expertise in the field. I especially want to thank Becky Grappo, whose work with international students informed the checklist; Marcia Simon and Joan Wittan for their valuable and authoritative advice about students with learning differences; Ruth Perlstein for her consummate exploration of Web resources; Shirley Bloomquist for the perceptions she brings to our college discussions; Diane Epstein, Shirley Levin, Gail Ross and Shelley Levine for the many spirited car-ride conversations on everything college-related; and Virginia Vogel, Lori Potts-Dupre, Joan Bass, David Gold, Jodi Siegel, Jean Baldwin and Emily Snyder for always adding to my knowledge of the college process. All these contributions have enhanced this edition, but whatever errors there may be, they are our own.

The encouragement and enthusiasm of Jerry Dincin, Peter Schneider, Susan DeJarnatt, Daniel Schneider, Leslie Reagan and Ben Schneider have been sustenance throughout this writing. We extend our particular thanks to Tom Vanderberg, our editor at the College Board, who saw the value of a new print edition and an e-book version and has had many valuable suggestions for improving the book.

This edition is as up to date as deadlines allow, but its currency about the college scene, its language, mood and spirit have been keyed in by the exceptional contributions of Paul Schneider, who attentively read and commented on the text. In fact, our whole family has played a big part in this edition, and so our loving thanks to Linda Kanefield and Irving Schneider whose thoughtful reading and discerning comments we so highly value and appreciate.

Acknowledgments to the Second Edition

It has been fun revising and writing this second edition. Since writing the first edition, I have benefited from the comments of the hundreds of students and their parents whom I have helped through the college selection process. Their insights and experiences on their campus visits have assisted me in making modifications to the original text, as have my innumerable campus visits during this time. It is not only this book that has changed; colleges and students have changed, and this book reflects those transformations.

Additionally, I have had the satisfaction of updating the book and adding the technology of the Internet to the experience of researching a college. I am most indebted to my colleagues at ACCESS, especially Ruth Perlstein, Nancy Rosenberg and Elaine Simmerman for their information about the "good" sites; and I also want to thank Susan Rexford, a skilled maven of the Web. My students, who have become masters of the Internet, were also of great aid, particularly Benjamin Schneider, who conducted initial research for me, and Eli Zigas who, first amongst others, told me about his experiences surfing college websites. I want to thank Lucretia Marmon for reading and suggesting changes to the original edition, Katherine Lacy for telling me about her detailed Web research, and Erika, Judy and Paul Fardig for reviewing my Internet resources and vocabulary. In addition to the many admission counselors who have been of great help, I want to thank Art Palms of Stanford, Stephen Schierloh of Sarah Lawrence and Judy Purdy of Wheaton (MA). The admission staffs of Haverford, Baylor, Washington and Trinity (CT) were most prompt and responsive to my inquiries.

The works of the late Abraham Lass, principal and writer, and the books and essays of the late Ernest L. Boyer, president of the Carnegie Foundation for the Advancement of Teaching, have been exemplary models. The philosophies, research and experiences of these educators have aided many people through the years, and I am particularly appreciative of their wisdom.

My family continues to be a source of spirited advice and encouragement, especially my husband, Irving, and my son, Norman.

I also hope that this book will please the younger members of my close family: Benjamin, David, Jacob, Max, Paul and Rafael to whom I dedicate this new edition.

Acknowledgments to the First Edition

I want to express at the outset my gratitude to Carolyn Trager, senior editor at the College Board, who conceived the idea for this book, with the hope that the results merit her expectations. Throughout, her gracious encouragement reinforced my enthusiasm for the project.

I wrote this book because campus visits and interviews have been central to my work as a consumer-oriented college advisor to high school students. *Campus Visits* is a natural outgrowth of that work and therefore owes much to the many students who used the suggestions and reported back on their efficacy. I want to thank all my students. I am especially grateful to Matt Zapruder, Ruth Polk, Eric Namrow, Nancy Clemmer, Mark Green, Cate Martin, Christine Rosenhauer, Ross Forman and Greer Mendel for their helpful insights. Several veterans of the admission process, now in graduate school and beyond, Eric Duskin, Jonathan Levy, Seth Grimes and Louis DeSipio, and others who are college bound, Ben Lewit and Joe Edelheit, contributed their constructive ideas.

My special appreciation is also due to many others who helped along the way. To the college admission counselors who gave so freely of their thoughts and expertise, especially Richard Stewart, Wallace Ayers, Carol Wheatley, Simone Stevens, Bonita Washington, Deborah Wright, Sarah Greenfield and Valerie Raines Bell, I am most grateful. I also want to thank that band of friends and specialists who contributed to various aspects of the book — Rhona Hartman, Maxine Krulwich, Barbara Mendel, Claire Sprague, Jane Lewit, Barbara Zelenko, Robert Gillman, Rhoda Wolf, Afaf Mahfouz, Gerrie and Len Pearlin, Rita Reaves, Mike Curzan and Gloria Stern — who were all so generous with their encouragement and suggestions.

I am especially thankful to Daniel Schneider for his ready assistance and expert research, to Linda Kanefield for her caring interest and careful reading, and to Peter Schneider for his enthusiastic support and wise counsel. There is no end to my indebtedness to Norman Schneider for his patience in teaching me the wonders of Agnes, my word processor, for his timely intervention in rescuing me from my computer mishaps, for his ingenuity in formatting the book and for his many helpful suggestions.

I am most grateful to Gail Forman, my friend and first line reader, who with sharpened pencil and practiced eye went over the manuscript, finding all my syntactical errors and nonparallel constructions. I especially value the devoted support and family advice of Dian Dincin Buchman, who was so instrumental in the formation of this book project.

Above all, few words can express my pleasure at having Irving Schneider at my side as my severest critic, best advisor, and valued companion. Throughout this writing he maintained his good humor and patience and was always willing to read, yet one more time, the pages as they grew into a book.

Of course, in the end, I alone am responsible for the contents. It goes without saying that I have attempted to ensure the anonymity of all persons mentioned in this book.

Zola Dincin Schneider

Part 1
The Campus Visit

Chapter 1

Deciding to Visit

There are many interlocking pieces in the college admission puzzle that involve searching for colleges, writing personal essays, filling out applications and then awaiting admission and putting the final block — the decision — into place. One of the key pieces to making this puzzle complete is the campus visit. This book provides details on all elements of the visit and interview to help you and your family get the most from your journeys to colleges.

Why You Should Go

Many students still choose colleges that their parents picked out for them, or ones closest to home, or ones that older friends said were cool or College Prowler raved about. But it is important to realize that choosing a college is a big decision that will affect lifelong interests, career and friendships. You should look for colleges where you can be successful academically, stimulated intellectually and happy socially — where you can learn, grow and make friends.

Just as a family of five shops for a large enough van for the whole family, not a two-seat convertible, you too should be looking for colleges that are *best for you*, not the "best college" chosen by a magazine.

To find the right colleges, you need to be a good shopper, especially now when a year at college will likely cost even more than a new car. No one chooses a car without a test drive, and no one should choose a college without a test visit. Looking at websites and talking or thinking about colleges doesn't replace the road test: the campus visit. A visit gives you a personal insight into the campus style, student body, social atmosphere, available facilities and academic dynamics. Visits to a number of colleges make it possible to compare them and to evaluate to what extent they match your requirements. Visits answer the questions a college shopper should be asking: "What would it be like for me to go to college here?" "Do I fit in?" "Will I feel comfortable and happy here?" "Will I get the education that I'm looking for?"

Emma, Diego, Jeff and Alexis, students at different high schools, all shared the same concern: Not one of them had any notion of what a college was actually like. They had read the vital statistics about various colleges in some brochures, looked at college websites and talked to a few friends about their colleges when they were home on vacation, but they still didn't know what a college was really like or how it felt to be on a campus and away from home.

Emma's first notions of a college came from listening to her sister and her sister's friends talk about their experiences, and each one wanted Emma to apply to the college she was attending. Although each made a good case for the college she had chosen, Emma knew that she needed to check them out for herself since she didn't think that what suited them would necessarily suit her. In addition, each of her sister's friends told her that her campus visit would be the biggest factor in making her choice.

Diego, a student at a large metropolitan high school, decided that a college in a small town offered few distractions and would therefore be more conducive to studying. Yet, when he made his visits to the colleges on his list, he was struck by how frustrated he felt at not having a wide choice of movies or ethnic restaurants nearby. He realized that although the students he met liked the closeness and togetherness of the college environment, he needed the variety of choices available in a larger community. To test out his revised priorities, he embarked on visits to his state university and to smaller urban colleges to see what they were like.

Jeff, on the other hand, had little idea of what type of college suited him. He thought that a small college would offer him good contact with faculty and he would get to know most, if not all, of the students quite well; but he also imagined that a large university would have a broad range of academic courses and social activities from which to choose. He decided that a serious investigation of different types of colleges was called for so that he could determine what best suited him.

Alexis's mother had always spoken enthusiastically about the wonderful education she had received at her women's college, but Alexis resisted the idea of going to a single-sex school. To placate her mother, she arranged for a campus visit and interview at her mother's alma mater. Much to her surprise, she found herself talking easily to the admission counselor about her reluctance to go to a women's college and her longtime ambition to become a lawyer. Afterward, Alexis stayed overnight with two sophomores, one from a small town in Georgia and the other from Chicago, talking most of the night about the advantages and the drawbacks of the college. They were frank and funny about a lot of the campus doings. Although Alexis and the two students came from dissimilar backgrounds, she was delighted to find that they shared an interest in vampire novels and funky earrings. The next morning she sat in on two classes and was enthusiastic about the give-and-take of the discussion. Pleased by what she was discovering, Alexis decided to put her mother's college on her own list of schools to consider seriously.

These four students were getting a good start on their college search. Sometimes high school students are so concerned about college that they forget that they control their own choices. You can and must determine for yourself which colleges are best for you and not choose a college because it is well-known or popular or on somebody's Top Ten list. It is essential for you to figure out which colleges match your needs, desires and aspirations.

Who Should Go When

Jim and Ann-Li, two junior-year honors students with heavy academic programs, were worried about the timing of their campus visits. Their top-rated colleges weren't holding interviews between January and June, not much would be happening on campuses during the summer and they weren't sure they could take time out from school the following fall. They talked to their high school counselor who showed them the next year's academic calendar and they saw that there were four autumn days when they could conveniently make campus visits. They compared the colleges' academic calendars and found that the colleges would be in session on those holidays. Aware that campuses are lively places to visit in the fall and that interview appointments are best booked early at the more selective colleges, Jim and Ann-Li got busy.

Mike, a varsity high school soccer player, hoped he'd make a college team. Because he practiced every day from mid-August through the fall, he had to plan his college trips during his junior year spring vacation or after the soccer season was over. He had been to several soccer camps and some coaches expressed interest in him. Luckily, when he called for appointments with the coaches, he found that the colleges were in session during his spring holiday and he would have a chance to talk to players, go to some classes and have his interviews at the same time.

Maria was the first one in her family who was college bound, but she didn't know if she wanted to stay close to home or go farther away. She wanted to make sure that her colleges welcomed Latino students and actively encouraged clubs and activities that served Latino culture. Even so, she didn't have the money to make personal visits to colleges. She talked about this with her college counselor and found that some colleges hosted "fly-in" programs especially geared toward first-generation and/or students of color.

Shawn, living in a depressed urban area, had heard about free fly-in programs from the College Track after-school program at his high school, and his counselor told him about Posse support groups in the community that help underserved students. His counselor also introduced him to Questbridge.org, which links low-income students to colleges.

Kayla had a strong interest in bringing clean water to African villages and had started a club to help raise money for these projects. In college, she wanted to combine on-campus environmental studies with courses about Africa and also have a variety of global experiences. She found colleges that suited her interests and needed to check them out.

Derek wanted to be involved in a sports-related career and found on various college websites a mixed array of possibilities: hospitality-geared, business-oriented, athletic/exercise science programs and communications majors. He needed to sort these out to see which direction he wanted to take and then find out what these majors were like at the schools.

On the other hand, Liz, a brass player in the school band, waited until her senior year before researching colleges. When she was a junior, she had gone with the band to Boston and had briefly ambled around Back Bay and wandered onto a campus. She had liked what she saw, but she knew she would have to devote much more time and energy to serious college visits. She reviewed the band schedule and determined some dates for visits when she wouldn't be involved with rehearsals or concerts.

These juniors and seniors were doing sound planning. Each student was devising a schedule appropriate to his or her needs, for there is more than one right time to make campus visits. The one essential factor, whenever possible, for junior and senior high school students visiting colleges is that the colleges be in session.

Getting an Early Start

If you live near a college, it is worthwhile to walk around the campus or perhaps use the college library for study or research. This would be especially useful during your freshman and sophomore years to get acquainted with the "feel" of a college. If traveling by car on a family vacation, you could use the opportunity to do a drive-through of a nearby college campus just to get a general idea of what a college campus looks like. Attending a summer sport camp on a college campus could be another opportunity to explore any of the buildings and facilities that are open and talk to college students who are there. It is useful on any of these casual visits to go to the admission office to pick up college information: the newspaper, a schedule of college events, brochures about academics, activities, study-abroad programs and a printed course catalog if available. Doing some of these things will give you an early start and take some of the mystery out of the college process. However, serious, in-depth looks should be saved for the junior and senior years when you're better able to evaluate what you see.

During the School Week

Juniors and seniors must be purposeful college shoppers. You should explore colleges when things are buzzing: when classes are meeting, students are studying and ordinary day-to-day activities are taking place. This means making visits during the school week.

High School Holidays

Junior and senior years are also intense academic periods, so it is important to balance high school requirements with college trips and schedule visits so that not too many school days are missed. High school holidays are choice opportunities for college visits. National holidays, especially those falling on Mondays when colleges are generally in session, are appropriate times. A good plan is to travel on Sunday and be on campus Monday. If several colleges are on the itinerary, Tuesday and Wednesday could be added. The early part of the week — Monday through Thursday — is ideal for campus visits because things are bustling then. If you are planning to schedule interviews, make your appointments with the admission office in the summer for the following autumn.

Spring Vacation

Juniors who have researched the colleges (see Chapter 8, "Surfing and Decoding a College Website" and Chapter 9, "Virtual Visits and Other Ways to 'See' a College") and put in the time to analyze their needs and requirements (see Chapter 13, "Putting Your Best Foot Forward") should go during spring vacation. Players of fall sports and students considering early action or early decision with application deadlines in November of their senior year should use these opportune holidays, but check well in advance to make certain the colleges are in session and that their admission staffs say it's a good time to visit.

Best Seasons

Late summer and early September before senior year begins are convenient times to visit because many colleges begin their fall semester as early as mid-August. Generally, fall through winter and sometimes early spring are the seasons when seniors should conduct their major explorations. But it may turn out that the only time available is during the summer of junior year, so don't miss out if that is true in your case. It's better to go then than not go at all.

Before Applications

Your campus expeditions should determine whether or not you will apply to the colleges, so make your visits before applications are due. Early decision and early action deadlines are usually November 1 or November 15, and sometimes a second early decision deadline is in December or January. Most regular decision application deadlines range from January 1 through March of senior year. You must plan accordingly. Colleges that have late spring deadlines may be visited later.

After Acceptances

You may decide to postpone visits until after you've received acceptances. If you apply early action, you will probably hear from the college in December with offers of special visiting days in the early spring. For regular decision applications, some colleges send acceptance notices as early as March, but many do not let you know before April. Keep in mind that if you wait until then you may have only a few weeks from the first week of April (when many decision notices are posted) to May 1 (the reply date specified by most colleges) to make your decision about which college to attend. Delaying your first campus look may put you in a tight bind.

Special Visit Opportunities

Colleges want you to visit. Many woo juniors and seniors with email, viewbooks, websites, Facebook and Twitter pages, merit aid opportunities and fast-track applications. Some invite students to take a special tour of their business schools or science labs. Other colleges offer intriguing alternative ways to visit the campus through group bike or boat tours, or through self-guided GPS or smartphone walking tour apps. Some have special "immersion days" during which students attend a typical class in addition to meeting with a faculty member and having an admission interview. Others "roll out the red carpet" for two-day visits and overnights.

Most colleges want to diversify their student enrollment and have instituted special admission counselors for students who are the first in their family to seek college, students of color, minority and international students. Shawn, Maria, Ann-Li, Diego and Kayla should be in contact with and direct their inquiries to this person. In addition to a special counselor, some colleges have set up a visit fund for students with financial need.

Ways to Go

Besides driving or flying on your own, Amtrak has a special discount for college-bound students and parents or companions. Some colleges have bus-in programs from particular cities with all arrangements made, and others have fly-in programs for students who are the first in their family to seek college and/or students of color, which may require an application. Other colleges will arrange to meet you at the airport and take you to the campus. These options aren't always listed in an easy-to-find place, so it's best to email or call the admission office to check it out.

When Not to Go

Steve and two high school friends took the family car on a warm summer Saturday afternoon and drove to the University of Santa Cruz, intending to get an impression of the place. They thought they would look around and talk to students and faculty about the way the college worked, take a look at the dorms, gym, cafeteria and science labs and pick up information. But look was all they could do. The college was shut up tight and all they saw were the outsides of buildings and the beautiful campus with its view of Monterey Bay. They had not accomplished their main purpose.

As important as when to visit colleges is when not to visit. It is bad timing to go during reading period or exam week when classes and activities cease and students are too frazzled to pay attention to visitors.

Weekends, though a convenient time for high school students to visit, are days to avoid if you want to see more than the party life of a college. By 4 p.m. on Friday afternoons, admission staff, faculty and students are keyed up for social activities and they may seem to be rushing their meetings with you. Visits and interviews are better scheduled for Monday through Friday morning. Few colleges hold Saturday classes, so you won't get much chance to sit in on them or observe the bustling life of the college. On Saturday and Sunday mornings, a college campus more resembles a deserted park than a lively community of scholars because most students, except for a few in the library, are spending those early weekend hours pursuing a favorite pastime — sleeping.

Don't plan to go Thanksgiving weekend or Christmas week when colleges are closed. Many students leave campus for the fall and spring breaks, so activities and classes are curtailed. Reading and exam weeks are not good times to visit, nor is late May when many colleges have completed their academic year. As every college organizes its own calendar, it is wise to check out specific dates so that you don't arrive to find the campus deserted. Admission staff may also restrict visits from the application deadline date to April when they are evaluating their current crop of applicants.

Keep in mind that it is one thing to see a campus on a summer's day when a mere handful of students wander around and only the admission office is open and quite another to see the full college in action. But if you are a rising senior and can only visit campuses during the summer, here are a few things you should do:

- Get acquainted with the admission staff, especially your area representative

- Pick up the viewbook and other materials

- Participate in an information session

- Talk to the students you encounter

- Take a guided tour

- Make an appointment with a professor in a field in which you're interested

- Stroll around the campus on your own and check out places of interest to you

- Take photos; make notes

- And, if you like, make an appointment in advance for an interview

Such a visit could also be a good beginning for sophomores and juniors to gather impressions and cover some of these areas, but for rising seniors it is a pale substitute for a visit when classes are in session and all the students are on campus.

It is always best to check your schedule with the admission office before you get too far into planning.

Traveling Partners

"It'll be great," Ted announced to his best friend. "Matt's up at Colgate and then we'll stay with Lisa at Hamilton and go on to Syracuse and Cornell. We'll have a blast, especially if we can get some other guys to go along and share the gas." The plan might have worked out except for one thing: Not one of the boys could convince his parents that it was a good idea. Their parents correctly questioned the usefulness of a trip based mainly on having a good time.

Friends

Making campus visits with friends is a fine way to see colleges but only if several conditions are met. First, don't look at the trip as merely fun; it is a major and costly undertaking, and having fun is an incidental consideration. Second, it takes planning and research to bring it off. If you want your parents' approval, you should present them with specific plans and a well-thought-out itinerary. That will help them to see the journey as a college shopping trip rather than a wild and woolly road trip. Going with friends has merit if the itinerary of colleges interests the whole group. Anne, for example, wanted to visit Wooster and Denison in Ohio and her best friend was interested in the University of the South and Vanderbilt in Tennessee. There was no practical reason for these two to journey together. To make going with friends worthwhile, it is essential for you to agree on purpose and destination.

The thought of traveling alone to Northwestern and the University of Chicago gave Nina butterflies in her stomach. She hadn't ever flown alone before and the thought of trying to get around in a strange city scared her. Her parents thought it would be better to make the trip with someone else, but no one Nina knew was interested. To solve this problem, Nina used Facebook to find another senior who wanted to make the same journey. Nina's parents also suggested that she call the admission staff, who proved most helpful by sending her directions and setting up a host to stay with on campus. The staff person also reassured her about staying with an unknown student host.

Groups

There are other partners to team up with to make campus visits. Some colleges, among them Oberlin and Mount Holyoke, sponsor trips from metropolitan areas for in-depth, two-day visits. There are independent businesses that take students on exploratory tours. Enthusiastic parents sometimes drive a caravan of students to a group of colleges, or a high school counselor may organize a trip. Frequently the school band, choral group or Model United Nations club will visit an area rich in colleges. You should take advantage of any opportunities like these whenever feasible. There are organizations like Posse and College Bound that form groups to take to colleges. Colleges, like Amherst, invite alumni children to attend special meetings with admission staff.

Some colleges — Trinity University in Texas is one — invite groups of prospective candidates to experience their college by including a campus tour, classes, interview opportunities, overnight in dorms, admission sessions and a chance to meet faculty and students. Others have informational open houses with one-day or afternoon programs, and still others have the already mentioned fly-in, bus-in program. Take advantage of any of these opportunities.

Parents

Many parents are deeply involved in the college process, but their students wonder if their parents should go along on campus visits. There are, indeed, advantages to their presence. Parents may lend both emotional and financial support for the venture and sometimes a more objective view. It is certainly a lot easier to manage a complicated driving schedule with the aid of parents. While your parents do the worrying about arriving on time, you can relax and enjoy the scenery.

When you are interviewing with the admission counselor, your parents can talk with the financial aid officer, or they can walk around the campus and gather impressions to compare later. Parents can play Dr. Watson to your Sherlock Holmes, all of you picking up clues that help determine if the college is a good match. Moreover, admission counselors are generally pleased to meet parents after the interview and answer any questions they may have. When parents go, they should arrange to stay in nearby lodging while you stay overnight on campus.

Cora certainly appreciated having her mother along. With two sisters and one brother, it wasn't often that Cora had her mother all to herself. The long ride from Virginia to colleges in Pennsylvania gave Cora a chance to tell her mother all about her plans and hopes for college. She found that her mother's good humor and reassuring perceptions helped ease her tension about the upcoming interviews. When interview time arrived, her mother quietly left to investigate the library and later told Cora what she had discovered. After Cora's interview, her mother had a chance to ask the counselor her questions about the college.

Of course, you know how well you travel with your own parents. Some young people feel that their parents will take control of the visit and influence their reactions to a college. For others, parents' enthusiasms set off a negative reaction and the students take an instant dislike to what their parents admire. If you have these kinds of concerns, it's a good idea to air them with your parents before planning a campus visit. (Parents: See the Afterword, For Parents.)

And Grandparents, Too

Grandparents may be only too happy to go on college visits with their grandchildren, as so often they have the best of the parental relationships. Grandparents tend to be warm, loving, noncritical listeners and can make the best companions on tours. Often they will have more time for touring than some working parents, and they may also have special insights that their grandchildren will accept more readily.

Going Solo

For some students, visiting colleges alone is the first act in the drama of "going away to college." There's a sense of freedom and a spirit of adventure implicit in the journey. For Emma it meant seeing a campus through her own "I's" only. Even though her parents' and her friends' opinions were important to her, Emma decided that her college tours were better done solo. She thought it would be easier to have casual conversations with lots of students and tour the campuses at her own pace without having a friend or her parents waiting around. She knew she would reflect better on all she had seen if she had time to herself to size things up.

✓ Checklist for Deciding to Visit

When to Go

❑ In fall, winter, early spring, late summer

❑ On weekdays

❑ During high school holidays

❑ When admission staff welcomes visit

Advantages

❑ Colleges are in session

❑ Students are available; classes are meeting

❑ You won't miss school

❑ Good reception

When Not to Go

❑ When college is not in session

❑ During exam or reading week

❑ On weekends

❑ When admission office is closed

Disadvantages

❑ Campus is deserted

❑ Students are busy

❑ Limited academic activity

❑ Counselors aren't available

Traveling Partners

❑ Solo

❑ Parents or grandparents

❑ Friends

❑ Groups

Advantages

❑ Adventure, independent look, freedom

❑ Emotional and financial support, second opinion; insights

❑ Share experiences, compare notes, companionship

❑ Prearranged by leader, group input

Chapter 2

Selecting Colleges to Visit

Nicole, a student at a large suburban high school, didn't know where to begin her college search. She made an appointment with her high school guidance counselor who asked her some questions about her interests and preferences, and then reviewed her academic transcript and testing record with her. Her counselor showed her a scattergram of where other students at her school with similar grades and scores had applied and been accepted. This gave Nicole an idea of her chances of getting in: the schools where she was most likely to be accepted, schools where she had reasonable chances of acceptance, and schools where her chances were more "iffy" because the competition was very keen.

Jeff, a varsity tennis player and fledgling photographer for his high school newspaper, was an average student with a solid college prep program, some honors courses in history and junior year test scores above the national average. He thought he had an excellent chance of getting into his state university, perhaps even the honors program, but he wanted other options as well. During the winter of his junior year, Jeff thought about himself and the kind of college he wanted, and certain priorities became clear. He realized that friendships were important to him, and he wanted to meet lively people from different parts of the country. He wanted a challenging education, both from classes and classmates, but one that wouldn't put him at the bottom of the group. He also wanted to play tennis, do some sports photography and perhaps join a fraternity. Like most high school students, he wasn't at all sure what he wanted to major in, but as his history courses had been quite engrossing, he thought that colleges with a strong history department would be good for starters. He still didn't know whether a small college or a large university suited him better. Jeff read a college guidebook, surfed some college-related websites for likely possibilities, emailed the colleges expressing his interest, and in the early spring of his junior year he sat down with a good map and his college list.

Tony was in a real quandary about his studies and planning for college. He had some difficulty with English and history, but he was pretty good in math and science. He decided to seek out an independent college advisor who spoke with him at length about himself, his interests and experiences. The advisor suggested he take an engineering aptitude test, and when he passed with flying colors, they looked up the course requirements of engineering schools. Tony decided to take on the challenge of physics and the Advanced Placement Program® (AP®) math course and to prepare himself for doing well in the SAT® and SAT Subject Tests™. When the results were in, he and his advisor drew up a list of engineering schools for him to investigate thoroughly on their college websites.

You must evaluate your academic record, analyze your needs and desires and research colleges before selecting those worthy of a visit. Soul-searching and researching are essential elements to determine college preferences. There are various objective, subjective and specialized guidebooks and directories to aid in the investigation and many websites devoted to the college search. Every college has its own website on the Internet to give you information. Many colleges participate in area college fairs. Collegeweeklive. com has live, interactive, chat-based events. Check your guidance office, library and local bookstore for books and websites that look helpful; see "Some College-Related Books and Websites" at the end of this chapter.

It is important to investigate all the colleges on your list, but it is of special consequence to make a real connection and know lots about the colleges on your list that you're most likely to get into. One of those colleges may be where you'll end up, and you want to make sure you'll be a happy student there.

In addition to deciding what considerations are important in selecting a college, you should also know what criteria the colleges generally use to assemble their acceptance lists. The checklists that follow suggest some preliminary considerations to use in selecting colleges to visit.

 # Your Preliminary Criteria

Selectivity

"Likelies"	"Possibles"	"Reaches"
_____	_____	_____
_____	_____	_____
_____	_____	_____

Type of School

❑ public   ❑ private   ❑ college.
❑ university   ❑ liberal arts   ❑ specialized
❑ technical   ❑ coed   ❑ single sex
❑ religious   ❑ historically black   ❑ minority

Location

❑ West   ❑ Mid-Atlantic   ❑ urban
❑ South   ❑ Midwest   ❑ suburban
❑ Southwest   ❑ Northeast   ❑ town
                                         ❑ rural

Size

❑ small   ❑ medium   ❑ large   ❑ megalarge

Cost (before financial aid)

Tuition and Fees $ _____   Room and Board $ _____

Academic Courses _____

Special Programs _____

Other _____

What Colleges Look At

- ❏ Courses taken and grades achieved: your transcript
- ❏ Grade point average: your GPA
- ❏ Rank in class, if provided
- ❏ Admission test scores, as required: SAT, Subject Tests, ACT
- ❏ Special tests: AP, IB
- ❏ Counselor and teacher recommendations; employer recommendations
- ❏ Application questions and essays
- ❏ Extracurricular activities
- ❏ Community service
- ❏ Summer activities/employment
- ❏ Special talents, skills, interests; leadership abilities
- ❏ Major or area of interest
- ❏ Personal interview
- ❏ Visit to campus
- ❏ Communication with college demonstrating your interest
- ❏ Ethnicity
- ❏ Alumni relationship to college
- ❏ Geographic location: where you live
- ❏ Family's ability to pay
- ❏ Special concerns: illness, disability, family issues

Source: Adapted from College Board materials authored by Jim Montague.

What Else You Should Do

- Surf college websites and click or email admission office to get on their applicant database.

- Familiarize yourself with college's academic courses, indispensable for a solid knowledge of what colleges offer (see Chapter 8, "Surfing and Decoding a College Website").

- Get an idea about colleges by surfing social media sites (see Chapter 9, "Virtual Visits and Other Ways to 'See' a College").

- Talk to college students when they're home on vacation (see Chapter 6, "Chief Aspects of College Life").

- Join a chat group at each college.

- Seek help from your school's guidance counselor, your parents and/or consult an independent college advisor.

- Attend college fairs and speak to college representatives.

- If college reps visit your school, attend the meeting, introduce yourself, and get the rep's business card.

- Talk to an expert in your field of interest to get suggestions and advice.

When You Cannot Visit

Julia felt left out of her crowd's college planning. Most of her friends were mapping out trips to Texas and California colleges, but Julia couldn't go. Responsible for all her personal expenses, Julia worked after school and on weekends, and she didn't have the time or the money to tour colleges that were far away from home. Julia worried that without visits she wouldn't learn enough about the colleges to make intelligent choices.

Hao's parents always wanted their son to get an American degree. All during his school years in China, he studied English along with the usual subjects and took the TOEFL and SAT to satisfy the test requirements. In his junior year, with the help of a certified international college counselor, he began his search on the Web and narrowed down his college list by using the "Tips for International Students" at the end of this chapter.

Indeed, there are circumstances that could prevent you from making any campus visits, and there is a limit to the number of colleges you can investigate personally; colleges may be too far away, and money or time may be in short supply. How, then, do you learn enough about colleges to know if you want to apply?

First, as already noted, evaluate your record, do some soul-searching and research the colleges. Heed the prescription above for "What Else You Should Do."

Second, follow through by talking to students who are at the colleges that interest you. You can do this online by joining the college chat group or subscribing to the college blog or by asking your guidance counselor for the names of students from your high school who are enrolled at these colleges. You may also write or email the college admission office for a list of students who live in your area. If there is a department, sport or extracurricular activity in which you are particularly interested, ask the admission office to put you in touch with like-minded students. Julia started an email correspondence with students in several art education departments to learn more about the courses and the students' experiences and Hao joined the international student blog at several universities. You should have your searching questions ready to ask (see Chapter 6, "Chief Aspects of College Life").

Third, take a virtual visit to the campus. Most colleges' home pages will direct you to their virtual tour. Be aware, however, that the public relations people designing these portrayals often show colleges at their resplendent best (see Chapter 8, "Surfing and Decoding a College Website" and Chapter 9, "Virtual Visits and Other Ways to 'See' a College").

Fourth, check out Collegiate Choice Walking Tour videos at www.collegiatechoice.com. These are independent videos shot on a real-life tour of each college.

Fifth, speak to college representatives at the college fair and during their visits to your school. Remember, you are shopping for a college that will best suit your needs, so ask questions!

Sixth, arrange for interviews in your hometown, either with alumni or with the college representative, or ask if the college does video interviews. (See Chapter 12, "Other Types of Interviews.")

Seventh, use social media such as College Prowler and College Confidential.

Eighth, join the college chat group and ask questions.

But after acceptance and before you enroll, make sure you're making the right choice by making an in-depth visit to the college you have selected. Nothing really substitutes for your own real, live visit. You don't want to be surprised by its size, its students or its campus. You have to make sure the college is a good match for you.

For International Students

More and more students from abroad are coming to study at American universities and colleges. Most international students are unable to make campus visits before applying. If you are one of these, take heed of the information in this book and pay particular attention to "When You Cannot Visit" in Chapter 1. It is also of great importance that you keep an open mind about colleges and not limit your research only to those that you have heard of or seen on a "best colleges" list. The U.S. Department of State's website (www.educationusa.state.gov) is a good place to start. You should also explore college websites and communicate with the international counselor at these colleges via Skype, email or phone to seek out answers to your questions. Following are tips for international students.

Tips for International Students

- Make sure the college or university has courses of interest to you

- Explore majors and career opportunities

- Look into academic global interests: courses or initiatives on campus and abroad

- Determine that college has a good retention and graduation rate for international students

- Check out number of international students, both undergraduate and graduate

- See if there are students from your country or area

- Find out if international students are welcomed and fully integrated into campus life

- Check out multicultural clubs and activities that also include weekend activities

- Join international students' chat group and Facebook site

- Make sure campus is a residential college in a safe neighborhood

- Inquire whether college is accessible to good transportation and airport

- See if there are food choices that comply with religious needs

- Inquire if campus or community has international food and/or restaurants

- Determine that international student office is accessible: returns emails and phone calls

- Find out whether college has special international student advisor available to you

- Check international orientation program for comprehensive, ongoing support services

- Ask if there is a Bridge or Pathway program smoothing transition into college

- Inquire if college offers an intensive English course to achieve proficiency

- Find out if there is a technical language course for your major

- Look beyond name recognition

Some College-Related Books and Websites

Listed below are some worthwhile college-related books and websites that have had lengthy staying power. Because the Web goes through changes every day, some URLs may have changed by the time you type them in. Remember also to check when the site was last updated.

College Search and General Information

Websites

www.collegeboard.org — A one-stop resource for college planning.

www.collegedata.com — Who's getting in where; matches, chances, admission tracker.

www.collegelists.pbwiki.com — Generated by counselors; excellent links to majors lists.

www.csocollegecenter.org — Center for Student Opportunity for first-generation and underserved students.

http://nces.ed.gov/collegenavigator — U.S. Department of Education statistics; data; college comparisons and much more.

www.nsse.iub.edu — National Survey of Student Engagement. Selected colleges surveyed for student qualities.

www.usnews.com/edu/college — *U.S. News and World Report*, College Compass, fee.

www.world-newspapers.com/college.html — College newspapers by state, city, college name.

Google: Common Data Set for [Name of College] — Admission data, ethnic enrollment and much more for individual college.

Books

Book of Majors. New York: The College Board. Annual. Descriptions and lists of majors; special academic programs in colleges.

College Handbook. New York: The College Board. Annual. Facts about every U.S. college, alphabetical by state. Admission, majors, housing, athletics information.

Colleges That Change Lives. Loren Pope. New York: Penguin Books. 2006. Forty student-centered colleges.

Fiske Guide to Colleges. Edward B. Fiske. Naperville, IL: Sourcebooks, Inc. Annual. Selective, subjective guide covering specific topics from academics to social life.

The Insider's Guide to Colleges. Compiled and Edited by the Staff of the Yale Daily News. New York: St. Martin's Griffin. Annual. Breezy and informative subjective guide.

Campus Tours Online

www.campustours.com — Virtual tours of selected schools, interactive maps, photos, links.

www.collegiatechoice.com — One-hour college tour videos by counselors. Fee.

www.collegeweeklive.com — Videos, chats for many schools.

www.unigo.com — Students review colleges. A personal point of view; some material is computer generated.

www.youniversitytv.com — Video tours of selected colleges.

Financial Aid and Scholarships

www.fafsa.ed.gov — Forms, calculator and more.

www.finaid.org — Calculator, scholarships and more.

www.meritaid.com — Colleges that offer merit aid scholarships.

Social Media

www.collegeconfidential.com — Videos, photos, student reports.

www.collegeprowler.com — By students for students; report card.

www.facebook.com — Every college and university has a page.

www.zinch.com — Information by college for students, alumni and admission counselors, with Q&A.

Chapter 3

Making Plans

Weighing the Choices

When Jeff sat down with a map to plan his itinerary of campus visits, he had his list of colleges in hand. He had divided them into three categories: "likely" schools, where he thought his chances of being accepted were excellent; "possibles," where he believed his chances were reasonably good; and his "reaches," where his chances were "iffy" and competition was keen. He resolved to study harder during the remainder of his junior and senior years, and he hoped to improve his test scores the following spring and fall, which would open up his options and strengthen his chances for admission.

His college advisor and his parents helped him evaluate his list. Of a dozen colleges, he had three "likelies," five "possibles" and four "reaches." Everyone agreed this was a good number and distribution for starters. He might add some colleges later, but eventually he would reduce the total number to between six and eight, keeping a similar distribution in the categories. His final list would represent a range of possibilities that guaranteed him a choice of acceptances.

Mapping the Visits

To avoid crisscrossing the same area on different visits, Jeff then put the colleges into geographic categories. He saw that he had three colleges scattered across New England, two in Pennsylvania, one in New York, four in the Midwest and his state university and one "likely" close to home. On his counselor's advice, he planned to visit his "likelies" to be sure that given the worst-case scenario he would have at least one college he wanted to attend. One of the "likelies" was in the Midwest where two of his "possibles" and one of his "reaches" were, making a journey there worth taking. As he didn't yet know what size college would be best for him, he included a wide range in his list. He realized that his best chances of playing varsity tennis would be in a small, less athletically competitive college, but that he could play intramurals anywhere. He would decide later where that fit into his priorities.

A look at the map showed that three of the Midwestern colleges were located within a 100-mile radius, but the "reach" university was quite a distance away. If he flew first to the city where the "reach" was situated, he could then rent a car and see all four. However, there were a few problems: Neither the rental companies nor his parents would let him rent a car alone; he knew he shouldn't schedule his first interview with a "reach"; and the trip would probably take four days, which might be difficult to arrange. He would have to work out another plan for these college visits.

The other geographic area that had potential was New England, but the colleges were widely scattered, and only by driving could he get to all of them. The two colleges in Pennsylvania were fairly close together and were another possibility. His state university and a small "likely" college were near home, and the New York college stood by itself. Jeff put asterisks next to those colleges where an interview was required or recommended and next to two "reach" schools where he thought his chances would improve with a personal interview on campus. The other two "reaches" had group interviews only, and he put a check next to each.

"Likelies"	*"Possibles"*	*"Reaches"*
State U — near home, large	C — Midwest, small*	H — Penn. small ✓
A — near home, medium	D — Midwest, medium	I — NE, medium ✓
B — Midwest, small*	E — NY, small*	J — Midwest, large*
	F — NE, small*	K — NE, small*
	G — Penn. medium-large	

* interview required or recommended
✓ group interview only

Getting There

Jeff discussed the chart with his parents, and together they made some plans. His parents suggested that the family take their vacation around Labor Day before high school began. In that way they could help with the driving and Jeff could visit all the Midwestern colleges. His parents reasoned that four days wouldn't be enough time for Jeff alone to scout four colleges, but by combining a family vacation with the visits, there would be plenty of weekday time at the colleges. Jeff checked the academic calendar to confirm that the colleges he wanted to visit were going to be in session. He then scheduled his interviews, making sure that his "reaches" came after he had some practice at the other colleges. When all the preliminary arrangements were completed, the family's vacation–campus visit plans looked like this:

Friday p.m.	Leave home. Drive to midway point: lake country.
Saturday, Sunday	Hang out, walk around town. Check out summer theater in area.
Sunday p.m.	Drive to college 1. Jeff overnight on campus; family nearby. Check vacation guidebooks for things to see.
Monday, Labor Day	College 1: Jeff's campus tour, lunch, classes, interview.
Monday p.m.	Drive to college 2. Jeff overnight on campus; family nearby.
Tuesday	College 2: same program as College 1.
Tuesday p.m.	Drive to college 3. Jeff overnight on campus; family nearby.
Wednesday	College 3: same program.
Wednesday p.m.	Drive to college 4. Stay overnight on road.
Thursday	College 4: same program.
Thursday p.m.	Jeff overnight on campus; family nearby.
Friday	Start drive home; arrive state park.
Saturday, Sunday	Hang out, go sailing on the lake. Investigate area.
Sunday	Arrive home.
Monday	School begins. Back to work.

The itinerary looked fine to everyone including Jody, Jeff's younger sister who was a sophomore active in the high school drama club. Jody searched the Web and read up on the places in which they would be stopping and found a number of sights to see and things to do. She made a mental note to look at the performing arts center on each campus they visited so that she would know a bit more when she began her own college search.

Although the trip had its ups and downs, overall the family judged it a success. They were pleased with the number of colleges they visited: just enough to compare and contrast experiences, but not so many as to create an overload. It gave Jeff the confidence to plan his autumn New England journey with friends, and Jeff's parents knew he had had enough experience to handle it well — they even lent him the car.

Jeff decided to visit the Pennsylvania colleges later in the fall on his own, reasoning that after the trip with his family and another with friends, he would have the know-how to interview at one of his top-rated colleges. Between his first and second semesters of senior year, when he had time off from school, he would visit his state university and the "likely" near home. He elected to wait until he had an acceptance before visiting the lone New York college. Jeff's counselor reminded him to check with his teachers about school absences and to take his transcript and résumé of activities along to the interviews in case they were requested.

Using Jeff's experience as a guide, you can draw up a list with specific points to follow. Make sure you arrange your plans efficiently so that you do not visit the same college, or the same area, more than once. You don't want to be like Louise, who never quite got her act together. First she visited colleges on a trip with her family, driving through college campuses without even talking to people. When she returned home, she read about colleges on the Web and in guidebooks, and whenever one attracted her, she persuaded her father to drive her there to take a look. Once in a while she would arrange an interview in advance. If the interview went well, she then planned on an overnight. In the end she visited some colleges two or three times, crisscrossing the same ground, spending lots of money and wasting time, not to mention disrupting her and her family's routine. The checklist on the next page will help you organize an efficient trip.

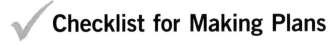

Checklist for Making Plans

❑ Evaluate yourself and your academic record. Get help from your college advisor and your parents.

❑ Think about your preliminary criteria and your priorities.

❑ Make a college list that includes "likelies," "possibles" and "reaches." Pay particular attention to the "likelies."

❑ Star colleges where interviews are required or recommended. These interviews must be arranged well in advance, as appointment schedules fill up early.

❑ Map out your itinerary. Plan for a full school day and overnight at each college whenever feasible. Limit each trip to no more than four colleges so that they don't blur into each other. (See "An Ideal Campus Schedule" in Chapter 4.)

❑ Check that the colleges are in session.

❑ Email the admission office. Make sure they know of your interest.

❑ Plan how and with whom you'll go. Make sure everyone agrees on the plan. If driving, take maps and plan each day's stopovers; if flying, know schedules of planes and connecting buses. Check out special transportation deals.

❑ Keep college visits and school demands in balance.

❑ Arrange for high school absence and plan to make up missed work.

❑ Pack appropriate clothes for weather and interview. (See Chapter 14, "Planning for the Interview.")

❑ Bring sleeping bag, toiletries and bath towel for overnight on campus. Take an alarm clock if you have trouble waking up in the morning.

Checklist for Making Plans
(continued)

❑ Take smartphone with camera and notebook.

❑ Bring names, email addresses and cell phone numbers of contacts on campus. Jot down interview appointment times.

❑ Bring questions. Take notes or email yourself your impressions. Use the "College Evaluation Checklist" in Chapter 10. Pack a good book or something else to do in case you get stuck somewhere.

❑ Take money for meals and expenses (some colleges give candidates meal vouchers and activities passes).

❑ Bring transcript in case admission counselor requests it.

Chapter 4

Making Arrangements

Admission Office Contact

Diego, who realized he would miss having a variety of movies and restaurants near the small-town colleges he had first considered, buckled down to his college "homework." He decided to do better research for his next round of college visits. After making a new list of colleges that interested him, he went to the library and, using the Web, Googled the cities and towns where those colleges were. He wanted to find out whether there were movie theaters close to the campuses and what kinds of restaurants were nearby. He also emailed the admission offices requesting on-campus and off-campus events. All this information would tell him much more about the college activities on and near campus.

Nora, a visually impaired senior, also emailed the admission offices to make arrangements for her college visits. She asked each office if an escort could be provided to help her on her tour. In addition, she requested that they send her the names of other visually impaired students on campus so that she could discuss with them the extent of the support services the colleges offered.

Having been a cheerleader all through high school, Margo was pretty certain she would continue this activity in college. She decided that during her visits she wanted to watch a practice session and talk with the squad. She made arrangements to go in the fall when the groups would be practicing daily.

Another student, Nils, was interested in acting and directing, but he also wanted a good creative writing and English department. This meant investigating college programs where he could get both vigorous drama training and a solid liberal arts program. He knew from a friend's experience that a good way to judge a drama program was to attend student productions. He emailed colleges requesting performance dates so that he could time his visits accordingly.

Addresses and Phone Numbers

To make a campus visit worthwhile, it is best to contact the admission office well in advance. Before venturing out, email or call the office to make arrangements. The addresses and phone numbers of colleges and universities are on each college website. Some colleges have toll-free numbers and these are often listed in the guidebooks. If you want to see whether a specific college has one, check with AT&T Information (800-555-1212), or look on the college's website.

Although queries may be formally addressed to the director or dean of admission, most inquiries and appointments are handled by the admission office secretarial staff. A prospective student's admission file is generally begun with the first contact of inquiry. While arrangements made by phone do not usually initiate a file, phone calls may be more convenient and allow for better coordination if there are several colleges to be visited on one trip. You should ask the admission office to confirm telephone arrangements by email, so everyone has their signals straight.

The admission office often has special perks like guest parking passes or chits for meals and will make arrangements for student overnights. You may email or call. What is important is to be in touch, and stay in touch, with the college admission office, as a great number of them log in your calls and emails, which demonstrate your interest. Remember to have a businesslike email address. Luvthatbeer@vmail.com is not appropriate; ltb@vmail.com is acceptable; better yet, Jeffrey.Miller@vmail.com.

On many college websites, you can directly sign up for a campus tour and college information session, while others ask you to phone the admission office for appointments. If neither of these actions is preferred, a short email like the following sample can serve as a model.

Sample Email

TO: Admission@burgess.edu

SUBJECT: Prospective Student — Jeffrey Miller

Dear Admission Office,

I am a senior at Endicott High School in Endicott, Maryland, where I am on the tennis team. I am planning to visit Burgess College on September 15th. I am hoping to major in history and have a tentative plan to meet with Professor Emerson at 4 p.m. and with Coach Wright at 5 p.m. I would like to take a campus tour and schedule an interview for earlier that day. I would appreciate it if you would send me your viewbook and any other materials relevant to my interests.

I look forward to hearing from you.

Jeffrey Miller

323 Crown Street

Endicott, Maryland 21048

Endicott High School

Jeffrey.Miller@vmail.com

When you return home, take a few minutes to thank the people you have met. Most colleges will place your emails in your admission file as a sign of your demonstrated interest, so your email correspondence should be polite and gracious. If something has particularly impressed you, mention it. College admission officers like to know what individual students find distinctive about their campus. Saying something specific about a college also indicates your perceptivity and highlights your interest.

Sample Follow-up Emails

[Email to college admission interviewer]

TO: PWaldo@admission.burgess.edu

SUBJECT: Prospective Student — Jeffrey Miller

Dear Ms. Waldo,

Thank you for the helpful interview when we met on September 15th. I learned a lot about Burgess and I hope you found out how well Endicott High has prepared me for college. After the interview and my tour of the campus with Henry, I had the opportunity to meet with Professor Emerson in the History Department. This conversation confirmed my interest in applying to Burgess as a history major.

Sincerely,

Jeffrey Miller

Endicott High School

Jeffrey.Miller@vmail.com

[Email to college professor]

TO: REmerson@history.burgess.edu

SUBJECT: Prospective Student — Jeffrey Miller

Dear Professor Emerson,

I really appreciate that you took the time to meet with me on September 15th. It was very interesting to hear about your courses on the Civil War and the contrasting military leaders on each side. My plan to apply as a history major at Burgess was definitely confirmed by my meeting with you and my visit to the campus.

Thanks again.

Jeffrey Miller

Endicott High School

Jeffrey.Miller@vmail.com

Checklist for Making Arrangements

- ❏ Check the college website or call the admission office to find out when campus tours and information sessions are held.

- ❏ Plan to stay overnight on campus.

- ❏ If you have a special interest, ask the admission office to arrange for a host with similar tastes.

- ❏ When possible, ask to stay with sophomores since they usually have enough experience to give you the range of information you want and are still close to you in age.

- ❏ Arrange an interview appointment. Ask for the name of your interviewer.

- ❏ Book your interview appointment far in advance, as admission officers fill their appointment schedules early.

- ❏ Plan to attend some classes that interest you.

- ❏ Get the course schedule from the admission staff for classes in a subject you're interested in. Ask if there will be a schedule handy when you arrive.

- ❏ Arrange to speak to a professor or coach.

- ❏ Check the schedule of events on the college website. Plan to attend a particular event that interests you.

An Ideal Campus Schedule

If possible, arrange your visit so that the interview is one of the last items on your schedule. This will give you ample time to gather impressions and information that will increase the value of the interview. An ideal pattern for a campus visit is as follows:

1. Arrive on campus in the afternoon

2. Take a late-afternoon guided tour

3. Join an information session

4. Have dinner and stay overnight with host

5. Attend a social, cultural, athletic or special event

6. Next morning, attend classes and walk around campus

7. Talk to professor in subject of interest; see coaches

8. Eat lunch and talk with students

9. Have interview

10. Take a breather and make some notes or text yourself some impressions

11. Leave campus for next college on itinerary

Some students may prefer to have their interview first, so that the interviewer might steer them to particular events, classes or places of interest. Decide which approach is best for you.

Chapter 5

Visiting the Campus

When Emma arrived at the campus, let's call it Burgess College, she was a little on edge. Even though she had read up on the college, studied the academic offerings on its website and talked to a friend who went there, she was still anxious about her visit. The admission people had been cordial on the phone when she arranged for the visit and interview, but she was leery about meeting a bunch of strangers who could decide her fate. She also wasn't sure what she should do first. If you are feeling as uneasy as Emma, not to worry; you'll be surprised at how welcoming the admission staff is.

The first thing to do on arriving on campus is to check in with the admission office. The staff consists of the office personnel and the admission officers, headed by the dean or director of admission. Admission staff see their job as a link between students and the college. They are there to welcome potential applicants and help them learn about the college.

Students and staff have a mutual interest: finding out if the college and the candidate make a good match. Providing prospective applicants with information is a major facet of the staff's work; meeting candidates and sharing their enthusiasm and knowledge is a favorite part of their job. Although the admission officers conduct the interviews and read the applications, their job at this point is to help candidates determine if the college is a good choice.

Emma's job was to be an open-minded and inquiring college shopper. As yet, she didn't know if she even wanted to apply to Burgess. She was visiting to pick up clues that would answer her question, "Is this a good match for me?" From the moment she set foot on campus, Emma had to be alert to all aspects of the college. At the end of her exploratory visit she would evaluate what she had seen and experienced, and only then would she decide if the college met her criteria for applying.

A Day on Campus

Emma started her detective work in the admission office, where she collected material on departments and special programs. To zero in on the ambience of the college, she picked up the school newspaper, the calendar of events and a campus map and was lucky to get her hands on the paper course catalog, organized differently from the academics section of the college's website.

The school newspaper gave Emma a view of the news on campus and the issues that concerned students. The paper also contained sports pages, ads for snack places, notices of coming events and personals. The calendar of events told her whether there were concerts, plays, movies, sports events, dances or special lectures on campus. Emma looked at the newspaper and calendar immediately, then tucked them away to take home and review at her leisure.

Emma also looked over the Burgess yearbooks strewn on the tables of the admission office and noticed that the students looked cheerful, spirited, and alike: The men had short haircuts and the women wore conservative tailored clothes. Most of the featured activities seemed fraternity or sorority related. Emma wasn't sure if that represented the majority outlook on campus, so she jotted down a note to ask students about it. The student guide arrived and was warmly greeted by the staff. Emma thought he seemed outgoing and good natured, and she wondered if this were true of everyone on campus. The office had an air of affability that was hard to resist, and Emma felt her tension draining away.

The small group of prospective applicants and some parents gathered in the admission office. The two other young women, one with a friendly, easygoing parent, seemed fairly relaxed. There was a pleasant-looking fellow who was traveling by himself. The other young man, with parents who kept nagging him, looked as if he'd rather be elsewhere.

Emma felt comfortable with this group as they followed the guide around the campus. She was totally in awe of the tour guide who walked backwards, always facing the group who followed his every step and word. The guide told her that students came from all parts of the country. Emma took particular notice of the bulletin boards and flyers. There were job postings and people searching for off-campus roommates. One flyer announced a poetry reading by a famous writer-in-residence, another reminded members of a meeting of the gay–lesbian group, another invited students to a gathering for vegans and yet another listed the schedule of the film society. "This place has it all," thought Emma. "But does anyone here ever study?"

On the one-hour tour, the guide enthusiastically answered questions and told a number of lively stories about the college. The group tramped by and through the old and new libraries, the science labs, the recently built fitness center, the theater and arts building, and the pride of the college, the new student center, which, besides the cafeteria, contained several snack areas, meeting rooms, a game room, an auditorium and the student mailroom. Crowded with students, it obviously was a prime gathering place. Emma noticed that these students didn't have the uniform look that characterized the students in the yearbooks. Bearded guys wearing jeans and hiking boots sat next to clean-cut guys in khakis and crewnecks; some women wore jeans and sweatshirts, some were elegantly color-coordinated, and some were dressed grunge style. "Anything goes," thought Emma, deciding that the Burgess campus seemed to have lots of diversity.

Special Note on Tour Guides

Campus guides are not all alike: some are lively, interesting students who are reliable spokespersons for the school; others may be less well rounded or informed. Some are so scripted and have memorized their text so thoroughly that it feels unreal. If you interrupt this latter type of guide, he or she becomes flustered and can't continue. Or you may run into a surly or giddy guide who doesn't know much. Or you may luck into the best kind, the one who speaks from the heart, is candid, and answers questions without hiding the true facts.

Schools that pride themselves on their individuality may present a special challenge to visitors. Their guides seem to have as a motto "Question Authority," and as a result they may appear negative or cynical when in reality they adore the college but won't admit to it.

Remember: The guide doesn't necessarily mirror the other college students. Try not to let the oddball guide influence your opinion. Don't judge a school solely by one student tour guide. Meet lots of other students to get a true picture.

After the tour, Emma followed a friend's advice: "Get lost," the sage sophomore had told her. "That's the best way to really find out what a place is like." With the campus map for security, Emma knew she would eventually find her way to her host's dorm. She wandered around the tree-lined, sunlit campus trying to imagine how it might look on a dreary, rainy day. She explored places the guide hadn't covered, getting directions from some students, talking at greater length with others, and all the time asking questions. She found the students helpful and friendly, and she savored her "lost" status.

Emma particularly wanted to investigate the psychology department. She had enjoyed psych in high school and thought she might like to explore the subject further in college. The following day she had an appointment with a psychology faculty member, but for now she wanted to wander around and meet some psych majors to find out as much as she could about the department. Getting directions from a pleasant student who welcomed her to "this offbeat place," she walked into the psych building. On the bulletin boards were several requests for student volunteers for eyewitness memory experiments, and Emma made a mental note to ask the professor about the projects. She saw that the departmental library was packed with students. People did study here!

Keep in Mind

❏ The sunshine factor: A beautiful sunny day can be seductive; a rainy day can dampen you and your interest. Try not to let the weather affect your judgment.

❏ No single person represents an entire college: Most admission people and faculty are helpful, but here and there may be one having a hard day. Don't be put off by one person who seems impatient with your questions.

Leaving the psych building, Emma walked across the campus to her host's residence hall, noting that it was a good 10 minutes' walk away. As she opened the main door and went down the hallway, she saw through open doors TVs, Xboxes, Wii systems and laptops everywhere. People were talking and some were listening to music through earbuds. Every door was decorated in a singularly creative fashion with space for messages. The hallway walls were covered with posters and colorful paint. Someone introduced herself and directed Emma to her host's room.

Maya, a Burgess sophomore who hadn't yet decided on a major because she was fascinated by just about every course she had taken, was waiting for Emma. She wanted to have an early dinner because later in the evening she was chairing a meeting on the lack of adequate night lighting on campus. She invited Emma to attend the meeting but also told her that there was a special lecture on stream ecology by a visiting zoologist, an ethnic dance club and a movie to choose from that night. Emma also learned that the main library stayed open until 2 a.m. and that there was a room for "all-nighters."

The two rushed through eating dinner in the dining hall, gabbing with Maya's friends who were all excited about the coming meeting and were already drafting a letter to submit to the administration. Emma didn't much like the watery lasagna, but thought the chocolate chip cookies were good, and she gathered that the dinner was pretty much par for the course. Food didn't seem to occupy the students' thoughts as much as the proposal they were framing. The group chatted long after their meal was finished, discussing the letter, their favorite courses, nightlife, best restaurants in town and upcoming campus events. After dinner Maya and Emma parted, arranging to meet back at the dorm later.

A friend of Maya's from lit class took Emma in tow to the ethnic dance group. At the dance, Emma ran into Jeff, the pleasant fellow from the guided tour. Greeting each other like old friends, they compared notes on their day on campus and agreed to meet after their interviews the following day to tell each other how things had gone. It was a great end to an interesting and fulfilling day. Both had prepared well for their visit.

The following checklist shows the features that Emma and Jeff covered to make their day worthwhile. You should do the same.

 # Checklist for Visiting

Pick up:

❏ Printed course catalog, if available

❏ Calendar of weekly events

❏ College newspaper

❏ Brochures on special programs

❏ Class schedule

❏ Campus map

❏ Host's name and dorm; where to meet

Look at:

❏ Yearbooks

❏ People in office, people on tour, people in dining hall

❏ People in residence halls

❏ Students

❏ Bulletin boards, posters, dorm door decorations

Make sure you have time to:

❏ Take a tour

❏ Go to an information session

❏ Have an interview

❏ Eat a meal

❏ Talk to students

❏ Meet with a professor/coach

❏ Attend a social, athletic, cultural or political event

❏ Talk to students in academic or recreational area of interest

❏ Stay overnight in a residence hall

❏ Use your smartphone to take photos and notes

Chapter 6

Chief Aspects of College Life

Emma and Jeff's college visits didn't end with the official tour and the overnight, for they planned to cover acres of campus territory the following day in addition to having their interview. Their goal was to explore the many facets of the college rather than merely look at buildings or judge the beauty of the campus. They wanted to find out what the college offered and whether it suited them. It was a serious undertaking, but each had a plan.

A college campus is a complex place to investigate with its interlocking subcultures, so it helps to have a system to find the authentic campus. There are lots of questions to ask, and you won't want to — or be able to — ask them all, but pick out the ones relevant to you. One way to accomplish your tasks is to divide your campus exploration into the five chief aspects of college life:

1. The students
2. Social life and campus activities
3. The academic courses and faculty
4. Campus facilities
5. The community off campus

Start with the student body to determine what kinds of students attend the college.

The Students

Friendships are an important part of your life in college. You will be learning almost as much from your close friends and classmates as from your professors and books. It is therefore crucial to get a clear picture of the students on each campus. You will have to decide if students are friendly, interesting, pleasant, smart. You must determine their academic attitudes, detect their social styles, discover their interests and enthusiasms and discern their backgrounds and goals.

Not exactly a piece of cake, but scouting for facts, analyzing your observations and heeding your reactions are your tools in this important quest. You're bound to base some conclusions on mere impressions, but if you keep your eyes and ears open and collect clues like Sherlock Holmes, your time on campus will be well spent.

Academic Attitudes

In assessing students' academic attitudes, you should evaluate their approach to college studies and intellectual pursuits. Get a feeling for how genuinely involved they are in their studies. Is learning an essential element of their college life? Ask students what the academic pressure and workload are like and how many hours a week they study. Do they seem bright? Are they alert and involved? Are they apathetic or drab? Is the college loaded with superior, average or below-average students? Will you be able to compete easily or with difficulty? Will you shine or be eclipsed? Jeff liked the idea of demanding studies, but he didn't want to spend all his time hitting the books. Emma, on the other hand, worked better in an environment where she would be challenged by the abilities of her classmates. Margot, another campus visitor, wanted a relaxed atmosphere where she could spend time on homework and term papers without sacrificing her social life and good times. Does the academic approach of the students match your idea of a college education? How would you fit in academically?

Social Styles

To determine the social styles of the students on campus, weigh their ways of having fun. Is there an appropriate balance between studies and good times? Do people work hard and play hard? What is the stand on the three D's: drinking, drugs and dating? Is there an emphasis on getting wasted? Does everyone hook up? Is there an identifiable "in" group? Is there a big rah-rah spirit on football weekends? Are fraternity parties a big part of the scene?

Investigate whether there are a variety of activities that provide social vitality. Find out if a good number of students participate in clubs and extracurriculars. There may be a proliferation of campus clubs, which either brings like-minded people together or fragments the campus. Margot wanted to be with students who shared her eagerness for the big college weekend, while Emma preferred people who liked movies and good conversation. Both talked to students to find out if the social style suited them.

Interests and Enthusiasms

Try to discover what it is that really motivates and excites the students. Do you get a sense of a fervent intellectual exchange of ideas or one of bored passivity? Do students flock to the movies, theater, concerts and art lectures? What is the focus of the school spirit? Is the talk centered on the opposite sex, the opposing teams or opposition politics? Are students bent on preparing for careers, are they thinking about job offers and salaries or are they looking for "alternative" lifestyles? Learn whether students share your interests or have others that might prove stimulating. Do you sense a strong school spirit on campus? Count the number of students wearing the college colors.

Backgrounds and Goals

There should be enough students on campus whose backgrounds are similar to yours to make finding friends easier. For example, Shawn wanted male and female African American students at his college to ensure a community of interest, Josh hoped to participate in a vibrant Hillel social life, and Mallory desired an active gay–lesbian group. Church activities were important to Karen, as she wanted to meet students who shared her religious values. Idealistic Warren didn't want to be left out in the cold without some soul mates. Isabella, who had never been out of her small town in the Midwest, longed to test her wings somewhere else but wanted some familiar types around for support. Ask questions to confirm that there are enough students like you on campus. Look around and see if you fit in.

However, you also want to branch out and meet people with different backgrounds and outlooks. Find out if there is a sizable contingent that hails from various parts of the country and the world. Do the students represent a variety of geographic, economic, religious, ethnic and racial environments? Is there enough diversity on campus to ensure a good mix? Most important, are these people with whom you can become good friends?

Appearances

Pick up clues from students' appearances to help in your evaluation. Notice whether the students all tend to look alike. Do they dress much the same as you do, or the way you'd like to dress? Do they look the way you want to look in college?

Clothes and hairstyles are sometimes pretty good indicators of personal style. On each campus Jeff visited, he compiled a "shoe review" by taking a rough count of how many students were wearing the same brand of sneakers or the same color and style of Doc Martens or hiking boots or flip-flops or the same trendy shoe. He figured that lots of duplication indicated a follow-the-leader mentality and little individuality. Emma noticed the number of pierced eyebrows, lips and tattoos; Margot looked for the preppies.

Similarly, you can take a survey to see if people are wearing identical shirts with the collars turned up, or if the majority of eyeglasses are horn-rims or wire frames. Are students dressed in the latest fashion craze? Can you pick up a sense of the students by the brand of backpack or brand of jeans? Are they into new-wave expensive or vintage? Do look-alikes predominate, or is there a variety of styles of dress and haircuts? Are there overcoats and down jackets, jeans and khakis, button-downs and flannel shirts; bushy heads, Mohawks, braids and shaved heads? Does one look prevail, such as jock or preppy, country or city, casual or dressy?

Conversations

Careful observation will bring in quality returns. Choose a spot to watch the passing parade, and listen to the conversations going on around you to capture a sense of the campus. What students are thinking and talking about tells you a lot about the vitality of the campus.

Some vantage points are the student center, any eatery, the library lounge, the bookstore and the mail room. What are students discussing; what are their gripes? Get some impressions from their conversational styles. Is the vocabulary arrogant or trendy or deadpan? Do they speak in preppy lockjaw or in street talk? Are they animated or groggy? Do they look terminally happy? What is the nerd factor? Are they discussing the merits of their courses or their cell phones? Are they talking politics or parties? Emma listened in on a group of students who were lolling on the grass debating the quality of the foreign film series playing at the student center and knew she had found kindred spirits.

Books and Bulletin Boards

Because books are the basics of college, notice which ones students are carrying. Are they reading Grisham and King or Gladwell and Bloom? What magazines and newspapers are in the bookstore racks: *Rolling Stone* and *People*? *The Nation* and the *National Review*? Unfamiliar magazines in addition to well-known popular ones? What are the favorite websites? What's the new viral video?

Get an idea of campus doings by checking out the numerous bulletin boards and posters. Are there notices for different religious clubs? Is there an African American, Latino, Asian or Native American student meeting scheduled? (See "Tips for International Students" in Chapter 2.) Is an LGBT group holding a discussion? Is there a political action planned? Is there an eating disorders meeting? Are the requests for rides home to mostly local places? Is the drama group holding auditions; the a capella society looking for baritones; the humor club seeking members?

Free Time

Get an idea of what students do in their free time. Are they involved in activities that provide opportunities to expand themselves outside of studies? Are they potting, puttering or practicing? Are they in the student center playing chess, video games or pool? Talking together or talking on their cell phones? Playing soccer or football? Sitting alone in the dorm playing video games or texting friends? What music is the present buzz?

By making extensive, personal observations while on campus and by talking with many students, you will get a better notion of the diversity of students attending the college. You will know more about their attitudes, their study habits and interests, their backgrounds, social styles and behavior. Think over what you've observed. Would you like to spend four years with these students? Would you enjoy being their friend? Jot down your impressions.

Social Life and Campus Activities

You won't be occupied with studies 24/7, so social life and activities become a significant part of your college experience. Cast your line and fish for clues about this aspect of campus life.

The best way to get responses to your questions is to chat with as many students as possible. College students like to talk about their experiences, and they have a yard of opinions about their college. Emma's opening gambit was,

"I'm thinking of applying to Burgess, but I'd like to know more about the social life." Jeff said, "I don't know anything about fraternities. Can you tell me something about them?"

The big social questions are: What do students do for fun? What happens on weekends? Do students enjoy doing things on campus or do many leave? Are there major campus events, such as a winter carnival or a spring fling that everyone attends? What is weekend social life like at a single-sex college? What's the party scene on a coed campus? Asking about the general weekend social scene will reveal lots about the students.

Fraternity and Sorority Life

Fraternities and sororities provide a readily available group of friends, social life and, often, housing for their members. The white-pillared mansions on and around campus are often home to the Greek letter societies. Talk to sorority sisters and fraternity brothers to find out what the main activities of the group are and what it takes to join. Ask if fraternities play an active role in the social life of the majority of students, or whether they are one of several social choices on campus. Are the frats and/or sororities cliquey or exclusive or do they invite all students to their parties? Find out if there are community service or academic expectations. Investigate whether the college administration has imposed limitations on pledging and rushing or on hazing and initiation rites. Does rush begin in freshman or sophomore year? What impact has this had? If you wouldn't want to join a fraternity or sorority, ask other students if you would still have lots of other social options.

Other Social Groups

Find out if there are particular groups on campus around which social life revolves. Are these groups formal or informal? Do they interact with one another, or does one group dominate life on campus? Are there cliques? Is it possible not to join and still have a busy life? Don't hesitate to ask.

Parties and the Three D's

What about campus parties? Who throws them? Who goes? How often and how rowdy? Are they straight out of *American Pie 2* and *Animal House*? When was the last toga or rave or theme party? Do students get hammered every night?

What is the predominant view on drinking, drugs and dating? Is there pressure to conform? If you don't drink, will you find similar people or will you be marginalized? Does the administration have rules and regulations regarding social activities? Do you detect evidence of special problems, perhaps from a newspaper story or whispers in the corridors? Has there been any recent event that has caused the administration to crack down? Emma found that one of the advantages of staying overnight in the dorm was that these hard questions were easier to ask when she shared a late night pizza with Maya and her friends.

Clubs and Activities

Find out if there are clubs organized around special interests and hobbies, such as politics, rock climbing, religion, singing or sports. What clubs sponsor campus-wide events? Are there signs of an active student government? Are there cultural activities such as movies, concerts, plays or art exhibits? Liz, who wanted to join the band, watched a rehearsal and spoke to other brass players to get the scoop on the conductor. Are there clubs and activities related to your interests? If you have a particular ethnic or religious interest, see if the college has clubs or activities with this concern.

Read several issues of the calendar of weekly events and see what activities are promoted. Investigate whether the activities are well balanced and supported by the administration and the students. What are the big sports on campus, and how much school spirit do the games arouse? Is everyone into football weekends, or are there other noteworthy activities going on even during the big game? Is this a college without a football team, and what does that indicate?

Connect with what you hear, see and read. There is luck involved in meeting people who will give you an accurate and balanced view of the college, but if you talk to lots of students who represent a cross section of interests, you will get a pretty realistic picture. Walk around. Look around. Take your time. What vibes are you picking up?

Academics and Faculty

The soul of a college is the quality of its academic courses and faculty. Before you visit, study the courses offered on the academics links of the college website to learn about the college offerings. (See Chapter 8, "Surfing and Decoding a College Website.") Check the Web for course listings. Email faculty in your area of interest. When you're on campus you can check out the validity of what you've read and also investigate other academic areas.

One feature to examine is the academic pressure and work load on each campus. Inquire about the kinds and number of reading assignments and the hours students spend on studies. If you're a bookworm and love the intellectual tussle, you'll have different needs from someone whose life doesn't revolve around studies.

But no matter what your purpose, note if emphasis is on course content or on grades, if classes are small with individual participation or if most courses are held in large lecture halls with students scribbling notes and doing little talking.

Are professors using clickers to engage the students; is PowerPoint overused? Ask about the general level of small discussions led by teaching assistants, or better yet, sit in on one of these sessions.

Find out how involved the faculty is in the lives of students. Are professors available only by email or can you have one-on-one conferences? How extensive are their office hours? Do faculty members attend sports events and/or invite students to a home-cooked meal? When you graduate, how many professors will know your first name? It's a good idea to get to know at least one professor well each semester so that when you apply for an internship, a job or a fellowship, you will have a choice of teacher recommendations.

The best way to find some of the answers is to attend a few classes in subjects in which you have some background and interest. Observe a typical freshman class and an upper-level course. Are students listening avidly or are they tapping away on their phones? Is the professor reading from well-worn notes without looking up from the page, or is he talking to and with the students? Does the professor take attendance with a clicker and what effect does this have on class participation and attention? Is the instructor interesting to you? Observe if there's interaction between the professor and the students and whether the students are prepared for class. Do they participate readily or is the professor pulling teeth to get a response? Is the professor having a discussion with one or two students or is everyone participating? Do the students sound knowledgeable or like show-offs? Do you get any sense of intellectual excitement? Consider whether you were stimulated by what took place in class. Would you be comfortable in this setting?

Inquire whether the college is changing its academic direction or retaining its current policies. Does the curriculum emphasize writing, critical thinking and reasoning with a stress on values and ethics, or does the college highlight career preparation? Is the college maintaining its academic standards? Have enrollments affected budget cuts? Have budget cuts affected enrollments? If so, what has suffered? Will it affect you? Will you be getting your money's worth?

If you are interested in global issues and study abroad, find out if any related programs are offered by the college and, if none, will you get credit if you go with another college's sponsored program? Can you get a joint B.A. and M.A., or do a double major? Will you have a freshman seminar with a small group of students? What other varieties of study programs are offered?

Ask questions about strong and weak departments, popular majors and what graduates are doing. (See "Checklist of More Questions to Ask College Students" in this chapter and Chapter 17, "Questions to Ask Your Interviewer.")

Another factor is the reputation of the faculty, not only in their scholarly fields but also as teachers. How do students rate the teaching quality in Rate My Professors? Have members of the faculty published any books lately? In what fields? You may find these books on display in the library or bookstore. Are some professors especially popular? Are they tough but scholarly, easygoing and real pushovers, witty or spellbinding lecturers? Find out who students think is outstanding.

What departments have renowned professors? Do the famous professors teach undergrads or only graduate students? Are the best faculty members teaching core courses and freshman seminars? How many full professors are women or minorities, and is anyone shaking the rafters about the percentages? Which are considered weak departments on campus? Are you likely to concentrate in these areas? What classes do students tell you not to miss before you graduate?

Many colleges have a student-sponsored and student-written course evaluation guide that rates the courses and the professors. Pick it up if it is available. It is an insight into students' opinions and experiences.

Campus Facilities

The guide who escorted Emma and Jeff on the official campus tour took his group into many of the buildings, but some guides may merely point out from afar the gym or the theater or the residence halls. It is a good idea to check out the latest upgrades of campus amenities: the new science building, food court, fitness center, library, dorms. Find out if any new construction is planned.

To get an authentic sense of the campus facilities, it is advisable to explore areas not covered on the tour. Emma "got lost" and found that a great way to scout around.

Housing

A good place to start is the residence halls. There are many varieties of housing arrangements at colleges. Some may have high-end housing with cleaning service and others may just have coin-fed washing/drying machines in the basement. As you tour the halls, check out the door decorations, the study and lounge areas and music practice rooms. Emma was delighted to see such magical and colorful doors with message-laden bulletin boards, and also practice rooms that were heavily used. What do you notice? Buildings may be one or more stories or even high-rise; they may be clustered or spread all over the campus. Housing may be coed or single-sex or the sexes may be separated by floor. There could be a choice of a single or double room or a suite shared by three or four. There may be dorms for freshmen only with assigned roommates or dorms where all the classes live together and the choices are yours. See if the lounges are crowded or unused. Find out if there is on-campus housing for all four years, if there is a problem with overcrowding, or if you may live in off-campus housing. If you might be an honors student, will you have special housing?

In addition, there may be special-interest dorms, such as a French house where only French is spoken, or theme dorms with a particular academic focus, or a co-op house where food expenses and activities are shared. You may find all the campus athletes live in a dorm that is as exclusive as a frat. Some dorms may be so noisy that you'll need a refuge for quiet study; others may be substance free, or focused on health and wellness or on living green.

At some colleges, there may be a residential college system in which students live in independent facilities, provided with their own dining halls and special activities, under the supervision of a faculty housemaster. Find out what your housing options are on each campus and look at housing for juniors and seniors off campus.

Investigate the living quarters and see if there is enough space to move around and sufficient wiring for all your electronic stuff. "The 21st-century rule of thumb," says the executive director of a college housing association, "is a port per pillow," though many colleges are switching to Wi-Fi instead of Ethernet connections. Check to see if the rooms are set up with wireless or high-speed Internet access and premium cable TV. Does the college limit your access to the cloud? See also if the furniture is built in, nailed down or movable. Are there sufficient closets and showers? Is there a snack area in the building or a refrigerator handy? Do students have small cooking appliances in their rooms? What types of lamps or electrical appliances are allowed? Where are the laundry facilities? And what do the insides of the rooms look like? Are they plush and attractively decorated, are they pleasantly unkempt with a hodge-podge of posters or just a mess without character?

See also if the common areas are attractive and well kept. A college that pays attention to its outside lawns usually pays attention to, and has enough money for, lots more on-the-inside educational needs.

College housing will seldom match the comforts of home, so get an idea of the pleasures or discomforts that await you. Bear in mind that where you live in your freshman year sometimes determines your college social experience.

Dining

Another area of more than passing interest is the dining halls. It's not only about food, but whom you eat with. Eat a meal whenever you can, but remember that no restaurant guide ever raved about college food, although many colleges are paying more attention to locally grown food and better cuisine. Find out what dining facilities there are, such as a food court or cafeteria. Is there also a snack bar, fast food and coffee house? What are the food plan options? Are there unlimited servings and a variety of options such as vegetarian, vegan, halal, low-calorie or kosher food? How late is the dining hall open? If you wanted something to eat at 2 a.m. on a school night, where could you get it?

Dining is more than eating. Many students linger long after the meal is over to socialize, so this is a good place to find the answers to your questions and listen to the conversations going on around you. Nils got the inside story on the drama department while munching on a hamburger, and Jeff discussed the strengths of the history department at the coffee and pastry kiosk.

Note also how far dining facilities are from the dorms. If it were snowing or pouring rain, what would it be like to go from bed to board?

Activity Centers

State universities, large private universities and some small colleges often have a student union or student center that houses many extra-curricular activities. In addition to eateries and lounges, there may be club and game areas with pool tables and comfortable lounge chairs, a music room, a meeting hall and theaters. Smaller colleges may hold all their activities in one building and larger ones may have multiple centers, so look for the location on campus of those facilities that interest you.

The student center, usually run with student participation, is where people get together for after-hours fun. It can contribute to the "good life" on campus and is often the hub of student activities. Check out the student center to see if its ambience appeals to you.

Athletic Facilities

Most colleges have extensive sports facilities. Notice if the gym is open at all times to everyone or if varsity sports have priority. Does the fitness center have enough treadmills? Is it state of the art or run-down? Can you play squash or racquetball whenever you want? Are there pick-up soccer and basketball games? Is there an indoor track and pool? Is there a climbing wall that students swarm to? Emma asked if the pool was open to lap swimmers at particular hours; Jeff counted the tennis courts. Does the college have crew, and where do they practice? What share of the facilities is for women's sports? Have any sports been dropped or are there plans to do so? Will this affect you?

The college should have varying levels of activity to accommodate interested students of different abilities so that no one is eliminated because the level is too high or too low. This is important not only in sports but in all other recreational activities as well. Emma thought it would be fun to try out for a play, but because she had never acted before she wanted to find an appropriate group for her fledgling effort. She walked into the theater to talk to the group rehearsing for a show to ask about the various groups that put on plays.

Health, Personal Counseling, Career Services

Colleges usually have a health center and often an infirmary with some allied medical professional on call. An exchange student named Jim had asthma, and occasionally needed an emergency shot. He checked whether the college itself handled special problems, or whether he would have to get outside help.

Inquire about the health services. Everyone goes through some stress at college, often relieved by talking to the Resident Advisor (RA), who is usually an upperclassman living on the hall. There are also mental health counselors who meet with students by appointment and help with difficult emotional experiences. In the health or fitness center there may be an office that provides services and tackles problems related to the physical and emotional concerns of students, such as eating disorders, safe sex, sexual assault prevention, and drinking and drug issues, in addition to problems that arise with roommates or concerns with family. As you might expect, larger universities often offer a wider range of such services than smaller colleges that haven't been faced with as many diverse problems. Look into how students rate the services. (See Chapter 7, "Checklist for Students with Emotional Needs.")

See if there is a career counseling and placement office on campus. Lots of students like Luke might know the direction they want to take in college, but most young people are unclear about what they want to do five or 10 years down the road. They know they want to expand their horizons, meet students with whom they can become good friends and have an interesting, fun time in college. But they also want to get a better direction to their lives. The career counseling service is the place to look. Find out if it serves a useful function for students. Does the college encourage job interviews on campus? Where are the prep courses for the GRE, MCAT or LSAT? Does the college also sponsor a program for minority students? Do many students enter the Peace Corps, AmericaCorps or Teach For America?

Special Student Services

Special students, such as the hearing and visually impaired, the wheelchair-bound, the learning disabled, should inquire into the services that colleges provide for their particular needs. Is there an office that handles special services or an organization on campus that is attuned to special needs? Does the college provide readers or adaptive equipment for the visually impaired; is there wheelchair access to all parts of the campus; are there interpreters for the hearing impaired? Does the campus provide supervised housing or private housing off campus? (See Chapter 7, "If You Have Special Needs" and the Checklists).

Campus Security

Everyone wants to feel safe on campus, so students should check to see what campus security is like. You would do well to explore the campus and see if the walkways from dorms to library, from classes to dorms, from eateries to home base are well lighted. Are there emergency phones strategically placed around the campus? Does the college maintain an adequate security staff for the needs of the students? Is there special monitoring in the residence halls; do students need an ID to get into the dorms? Does the college provide a bus or an escort service for late-hour assistance? Does the schedule overlap with library and lab hours? You should ask if there have been any recent incidents that caused alarm and whether the college is handling the problem to the satisfaction of the students. Campus Crime reports are required by the Campus Security Act and are generally available through the admission office. Emma's contact with her host, Maya, made her aware that the lighting conditions at Burgess needed attention and that Burgess students were actively involved in improving the situation.

Women may want to get in touch with the women's center, which often sponsors educational programs on women's issues, such as date rape. The center is a good place to ask about recent incidents that involved women's safety problems. Policy statements and campus social codes are often on the college website.

Computers and Tablets on Campus

Other factors strongly worth looking into are the computer, electronic and Internet facilities and services on campus. Are there state-of-the-art facilities on campus, and, if not, are there plans afoot for modernization? Is the college switching from computers to tablets for student use? Is there access to sufficient computer time at an adequate number of terminals? What are the hours of the computer rooms, and are they scattered over the campus in addition to the ones in the library? Are the dorms set up for high-speed wireless access? You might want to look into the policy on email accounts, blogs and wireless networks. Is there access to all these facilities for off-campus and commuting students? Is the college using smartphones, tablets and apps for teaching and general communication? If you don't have a compatible device, does this affect your contact with the professor? Big technology changes are taking place. Some professors are banning tablets and laptops in classrooms; others want you to have them. Will this affect you?

The Library

Many students spend lots of time in the library, so look it over. Is the staff courteous and helpful? What are the hours? Is there a room for "all-nighters"? You can assume that if the library stays open way into the night weekdays and weekends and is crawling with students, you are on a hard-working, serious campus.

See if the book stacks are open for browsing or closed, which means going to the online catalog first. Are there enough computers for all who need them? Is the information technology up to speed? Are students reading in small carrels tucked away in the stacks? What are the physical conditions of the library? Are the main rooms comfortable? Is there sufficient seating, or does the library seem overcrowded? Is there a good balance of long tables, private spaces and study rooms? Is there also a lounge where students meet between bouts of hard study? Is there a food concession? Ask if the library is a good place for study and research. Are there long lines at the copy machines? See if there are departmental libraries and special collections open to students and if they have current periodicals. What books by faculty are on display? Ask students what their experiences have been. Do they give the library a good rating?

Additional Areas

Kiyo, a serious science student, wanted to find out more than if the lab equipment was up-to-date. She knew that many universities desired to be on the cutting edge of science research and were spending big bucks to get there. She wished to know if this was true at the colleges she was visiting. She was lucky to get into a special tour of the science buildings.

Walk into the campus bookstore and see what is being sold in addition to textbooks. It may carry a full complement of out-of-town newspapers, special-interest magazines and bestsellers along with the college T-shirts. Does it also have a line of drugstore items and other necessities? Does it sell batteries and lip balm?

As you amble about the campus, note the layout and the buildings. Do students find it convenient to get from classes to the dining hall and from the library to their dorms? Are the buildings both old and new and in good shape? Is there an architectural style and unity to the campus that's appealing? Are the grounds well kept? Good maintenance is one indication of sufficient funding in the budget for the college's well-being.

There may be a host of other places to see on campus such as an art museum, or perhaps a special library, historic sites or exhibits and concerts to go to. If your family is making the visit with you, these may be places for them to see while you interview or scout the campus on your own. Jeff's family had a fun time seeing all the sights and Jody, his high school sophomore sister, loved seeing a production of *Les Miz*.

Investigate the liaison between students and the administration. Find out what role students have in decision making. Is the student government an effective voice for the students or did the students have to stage a sit-in to obtain their demands?

The Community Off Campus

Some colleges are like small cities, containing everything you want for a stimulating life; others depend on the community outside the campus to fulfill needs; and still others may not have enough activity on or off campus. Weigh the college and the community activities to decide whether there is a winning combination for you. The liveliness of the college and the surrounding community can be a big factor in your enjoyment of your four college years.

You want to ask, "Is there life outside the campus?" Find out how far away town is and how to get there. Can you walk or will you need your bike or a car? Is there a bus or do students rely on other students who have cars? How do students generally get to town? What exactly is that community: a couple of streets with college-related stores, a suburban area with a shopping mall or a booming city?

If you didn't want to go to any events on campus, could you find something to do in town? If the college has a guide to places and activities off campus, pick it up. Buy the local newspaper. Are there restaurants and a multiplex; theater; concerts and museums; bars and pizza places; ice cream parlors and McDonald's? Is there a place to dance or listen to music? If you needed a skirt, shirt, sweats or shoes, where could you buy them?

Do the students and the town have anything to do with each other? Is there cooperation or friction with the community? Do students and townspeople join together in an anti-litter drive or campaign for local politicians? Do students do volunteer work or tutor in the local school? Zack was particularly interested in the volunteer work that students could do. Could you find a paying job in the community? Do students stay in the area after graduation?

When you get home, you can do an online check of the chamber of commerce or similar sites and look into Chowhound, Yelp or Menu Pages.

You should also consider how far the college is from home, how long it will take to make the journey, how much it will cost and alternative means for getting from home to college. Remember that greater distances sometimes take less time because you fly rather than drive or take a bus.

Checklist for Exploring College Life

Area to Research	What to Look For	How or Where to Look

Students	Academic attitudes
	Social styles
	Interests
	Backgrounds
		Talk to students and listen to
		   their conversations;
		   observe those passing by
		Go to student center
		Look at bulletin boards
		Browse Facebook, other
		   social media
		Examine photos online
		Ask admission counselor

Social Activities	Parties, athletic and cultural
	events, clubs
		Visit YouTube, Facebook, and
		   CollegeProwler
		Read bulletin boards and
		   posters, calendar of
		   events, newspaper
		Talk to students
		Attend events

Academics	Quality Pressure, competition Workload Emphasis	Sit in on classes Talk to students Study print or online course catalog Browse social media sites
Faculty	Reputation Quality Availability Involvement	Talk to students Sit in on classes Browse college website Check out Rate My Professors website Read student course guide

Checklist for Exploring College Life
(continued)

Area to Research	What to Look For	How or Where to Look
Campus Facilities		
❑ Housing	Varieties, location	Visit residence halls; take online tour
❑ Dining	Options, quality	Eat at dining hall
❑ Activity Centers	Liveliness, range of activities	Go to student center; visit online
❑ Athletics and Recreation	Range, hours	Go to gym, pool, fitness center; take virtual visit
❑ Health and Special Student Services	Usefulness, range, support	Talk to students and counselors; use online resources
❑ Miscellaneous	Theater, arts center, book-store, etc.	Look, ask questions; browse social media sites
❑ Library	Hours, comfort, lighting; reputation	Visit, talk to students; take virtual visit
Off Campus Community	Activities Entertainment Shopping Town/gown relations	Go into town Buy local newspaper Talk to students and admission staff Browse chamber of commerce website

Checklist of More Questions to Ask College Students

About the College's Reputation

❏ Has the college lived up to your expectations?

❏ Has anything been a major disappointment?

❏ Was anything surprising to you?

❏ Is the evaluation on Web, in magazines and books fair, accurate and up to date?

❏ Do you think the information on CollegeProwler and College Confidential or social media sites is accurate?

❏ What is special about this college? What are its strengths?

❏ Are there any particular tensions on campus?

❏ Is there something special I should see before I leave?

❏ Have you been happy here? What would you change if you had the chance?

❏ If you were to do it all over again, would you still choose this college?

About Housing

❏ Does the housing system satisfy students?

❏ Is it quiet enough to study in the dorms?

❏ Which residence halls are good places to live in?

❏ Do the special houses succeed in what they attempt?

About Activities

❏ How are intramural sports organized? By dorm? By luck?

❏ How do I qualify for the newspaper? Orchestra? Choral group? Radio station'? Drama group? (Substitute your special interest.)

❏ Is it easy to form a new club?

❏ What were some social, political or academic issues that concerned students last year? How did the administration react? What was the result?

Checklist of More Questions to Ask College Students

(continued)

About Academics and Faculty

❑ What required courses are taught by professors? By teaching assistants?

❑ How many hours a week do students typically study?

❑ How easy is it for freshmen to get the classes they want? Sophomores?

❑ Do students have difficulty getting into their required courses when they want to?

❑ Which classes for freshmen are usually large?

❑ Is it easy to get to know professors?

Covering the Spectrum

By inquiring about the students, the social life, academics, campus facilities, and the community outside the campus, you will accumulate vital knowledge about the college and its campus life. You then can determine whether the college matches your personality, interests and needs. Can you grow and change and still love the college?

Take notes as you go along; heed your gut reactions. Remember that although your student host is a rich source of information, you shouldn't rely too heavily on one person. Emma found it helpful to stay with a sophomore who had a year's experience under her belt and had gotten over her freshman fears. Jeff stayed with an older junior who had experienced both the highs and lows of college life. But both talked to many people in addition to their hosts to get a balanced view of Burgess. You must aim for the same.

Once you are home you may find yourself filled with sights and sounds of the college you visited and unsure of how to sort out your impressions. The checklists in this chapter and in Chapter 10 will provide you with a framework to organize your impressions.

Chapter 7

If You Have Special Needs

Some Special-Needs Students

Penny, who had always thought of herself as a slow and struggling student, was diagnosed late in her sophomore year with a hearing deficit. With her documentation, she received an Individual Education Plan (IEP) that gave her teachers' notes. Although she had to study much harder than her classmates, she became a better student and was able to take AP classes where she did high-quality work. She began to see herself in college. She recognized that in college she would have to sit in the front row of every class and she also would need note-taking accommodations to achieve her potential.

Ethan was different from other kids. He avoided looking at or playing with other youngsters and communicated only with his family. As he grew older, he became obsessed with train schedules and thought mostly in mathematical terms. In his small private school, the teachers took his personality into account, found that he was unusually gifted in math, and that with their special encouragement, he could learn other subjects as well. They helped him expand his interests and, in junior year, he began to write with greater ease. His test scores showed that he was good college material. He and his family knew that he would need special accommodations if he were to make it in college, and they were also concerned about the campus social environment in which he would feel comfortable.

As a gymnast always seeking perfection, Alyssa became bulimic in high school and twice had to be hospitalized. With her therapist and parents supporting her, she began her college search, knowing that she would need some emotional backup at the start of her college years.

All during school, Carl sat in the back of the room and fidgeted, trying to pay attention to his teachers, but he wasn't able to focus for long. He had difficulty understanding books unless he read very slowly. In class, he couldn't wait to be called on and blurted out his answers. His academic problems increased in high school when he couldn't take legible notes, struggled with writing and forgot assignments. After his school counselor recommended testing, he was diagnosed with ADHD with a learning disability. Carl was immensely relieved to find out that he wasn't stupid, but that there was a medical basis for his difficulties. He began doing better work with the aid of medication, organizational help and some tutoring, and he knew he would need a variety of support services in college.

Penny, Ethan, Alyssa and Carl were students with special needs.

In addition to paying heed to the previous chapters, if you are a student with special needs you have to investigate the resources you will require to be successful on campus. This demands particular exploration of the special services that the college may offer. The staff should be eager, informative and imaginative about plans to integrate you into the life and community on campus. It is important to gauge the attitude of the staff as their welcome and willingness to help is essential for ensuring that you achieve your goals. It will tell you a lot about the attitude, availability and interest if the office for special needs is in an easy-to-get-to area, open and inviting, or hidden in an out-of-the-way basement.

In almost all cases, colleges with special disability services require recent documentation to justify the requisites for particular accommodations. Colleges that work with special-needs students will often have an office for disability services that details online what services they offer and what documentation they require. It is best to look into this before arranging a visit. If the college is legally but only minimally compliant with the Americans with Disabilities Act and you need more than mere compliance, this school may not be appropriate for you.

It is critical that when you apply for accommodations you understand the nature and impact of your disability in the classroom setting. You should know what accommodations you require for specific situations, recognize your strengths and weaknesses and assume responsibility for yourself. You must learn to be proactive and take up the challenge of being in college. When you learn how to advocate for yourself you will be most effective in obtaining the help you need. Your parents aren't going to be at your side hour to hour or day to day, although they certainly could be there at the initial meetings with the special-needs counselor. Whenever possible, you should take charge in these encounters by having a list of required needs and questions about the program. Your parents should try to remain in the background. If you have an oral communication difficulty, much of this can be done through email.

There are other special-needs students who fall under a rubric different from the disability office. These may be students with psychological issues or those recovering from an addiction. Other students might need limited tutoring, personal or career counseling or adaptive sports. These needs are covered in a variety of offices, such as the health and counseling center or writing skills and math centers. The office of disability services may also be involved, as some students need support in more than one area.

The following pages provide advice and checklists for students with learning disabilities, students with emotional needs, and students with physical needs.

Students with Learning Disabilities

To request special services, it is important to obtain appropriate documentation and present it to the office of disability services at the college. Colleges usually want to see psycho-educational or neuropsychological testing reports, no more than three years old. Some colleges may look at the Individual Education Plan or the 504 Plan detailing what the high school has done to make reasonable accommodations, but this is generally not a substitute for up-to-date testing.

✓ Checklist for Students with Learning Disabilities

❑ Obtain appropriate documentation, as specified by college

❑ Meet with special services counselor to discuss needs before deciding on a college

❑ Investigate how long the program has been in place, how many students are accommodated

❑ Find out how many professional learning specialists are available

❑ Ask about the success rate of program: retention and graduation rate of learning disabled (LD) students

❑ Find out how accommodations are delivered and how often students need to request them

❑ Ask if there is a fee for service

❑ Check out possible accommodations and arrangements to secure services

Accommodations available on a case-by-case basis may include:

❑ Note taker or note-taking pen

❑ E-text, recorded or scanned textbooks

❑ Priority registration, course substitutions or waivers, remediation

❑ Test accommodations: oral tests, reader, scribe, extended time, quiet room

❑ Use of laptop, calculator, digital recorder, reading pens, other devices

❑ Voice-activated dictation software

❑ Outlining or writing software

✓ **Checklist for Students with Learning Disabilities**
(continued)

❑ Portable keyboards

❑ Availability of Kurzweil 3000 or similar text-to-speech software

❑ Other adaptive technology and technology assistance

Other support services that may assist students with learning disabilities include:

❑ Tutoring, professional or peer

❑ Writing, math or other academic support center

❑ Supplemental instruction

❑ Mentoring program

❑ Coaching or one-on-one meetings for organizational support, study skills

❑ Workshops or seminars for LD students

❑ Individual academic advisor who understands LD issues

❑ Social support through individual or group meetings

To gain further insight:

❑ Meet with a student who has used similar services and check out ease and effectiveness of the accommodation

❑ Check out blogs for LD students and join chat

❑ Find out if LD students are fully integrated into the college and its social life

Students with Physical Needs

Many students enter college with disabilities, for example, visual or hearing impairment, or epilepsy, polio, muscular dystrophy or other medically significant issues that require special accommodations. These are usually covered by ADA and Section 504 of the Rehabilitation Act. If you have severe but less common disabilities, it is especially relevant to learn whether the personnel you encounter are willing to make the extra effort to make you comfortable and to help you integrate into the college community. The college's office of student disability services will help you determine the availability of the following accommodations:

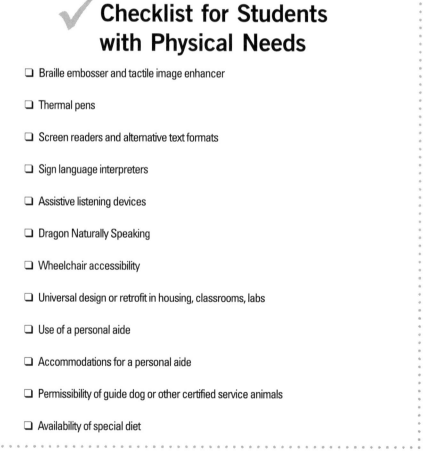

✓ Checklist for Students with Physical Needs

❑ Braille embosser and tactile image enhancer

❑ Thermal pens

❑ Screen readers and alternative text formats

❑ Sign language interpreters

❑ Assistive listening devices

❑ Dragon Naturally Speaking

❑ Wheelchair accessibility

❑ Universal design or retrofit in housing, classrooms, labs

❑ Use of a personal aide

❑ Accommodations for a personal aide

❑ Permissibility of guide dog or other certified service animals

❑ Availability of special diet

Students with Emotional Needs

Studies have shown that there may be a significant number of students who need emotional help beyond the aid of the Resident Advisor (RA). There are students like Alyssa who enter college with an ongoing eating disorder issue, others who may need medications, and still others who may develop problems in college, ranging from matters like a romantic disappointment, alcoholism or gender identity to setbacks that have led to depression, all requiring more professional assistance than talking it out with peers or the RA. Following is a checklist to guide you should you have the need:

✓ Checklist for Students with Emotional Needs

❏ Check out insurance coverage in family policy or college plan

❏ Locate health center and medical/mental health professionals

❏ Find out number of counselors and waiting time for appointment

❏ Check out how many sessions are covered in your plan and/or extra fees

❏ Investigate whether outside specialists are available in community

❏ Inquire about privacy rights

After You've Enrolled

- Introduce yourself to your professors and get to know them.

- Take advantage of professors' office hours.

- Meet with your advisor often.

- Make sure you know how to arrange accommodations.

- Use the learning centers and services on campus.

- Learn how to advocate for yourself.

Follow the Boy Scouts' motto and "Be Prepared." Preparation is a key factor in success, whether it is for class, for appointments with your advisor or in meetings with your professor.

Chapter 8

Surfing and Decoding a College Website

The college website is a goldmine of information that contains a treasure trove of features for those who have the patience to navigate through the site and separate real nuggets from fool's gold. This necessitates a lot of persistence as all college sites are different and their lodes of gold are in a variety of places, requiring you to surf, navigate, click and link to get the information you want. Because colleges are using their websites as an information-laden recruiting tool, you may have to decode and translate some of the features.

Window into College

At their best, college websites offer a window into a college. Keep in mind that you are looking through a stained-glass pane that the college has artfully designed to emphasize certain colors and hues to reveal its luster and sheen: its strong points and virtues, not its shortcomings or faults. Most institutions are spending hefty amounts of money to create entertaining, engrossing sites with pop-ups and changing scenes. These websites may be campus created or more often generated by an outside professional organization hired to promote the college to potential applicants and other interested viewers. The best sites are easy to navigate and dazzling to look at. Some colleges are more skillful at this venture than others, making the desired information available with just two or three clicks. A well-designed website can make the viewer believe that the college is better than it really is, and a poorly conceived site can make even a good college look inferior. In addition, some sites are difficult and slow and don't have easy links, causing students to become confused and frustrated. But two things are certain: college websites are always improving and what is there today may not be there tomorrow.

Cassie had her greatest rewards when she took on serious roles in her school's plays or when she sang in the choral group. She wanted to be practical about her college education, but she also knew she would be unhappy if she didn't have an opportunity to perform or sing while in college. She had to find schools where nonmajors could participate in these areas and where she would also find a full range of academic interests to pursue.

Tim was undecided about a major but he knew he wanted to go to a college that offered a great variety of courses, had a diversity of students and had good sports teams. He needed help in getting a list of colleges to research.

Carlos wanted to know if people from his state went to Abbott College and whether it had many Hispanic students. He first checked his school's college reference site and found that in the last five years only four students from his high school had applied to Abbott and only one had been admitted. He saw that the admitted student had grades and SAT scores similar to his. He went to the college's website and got lost in all the pictures and stories and tabs that he clicked on.

Zack wanted to go to a college that emphasized civic engagement and had nontraditional options, such as internships with inner city kids. He knew that many campuses now featured service learning, but he didn't know how to find them. He went to the Parkman University site and saw a picture of someone playing basketball with a youngster, but he couldn't figure out if that was part of a program at the school or just a good photo.

Anand, a computer geek and video gamer, needed to know if his colleges offered digital game design courses. He had to link into a variety of academic sites and sometimes into separate schools within a university's website to find related courses. No school seemed to have the information he wanted in the same place.

College Search Websites

On the other hand, college search websites, like guidebooks listing college facts, have the same organization for each college or university. Sometimes this is the best way to begin your college search when you are looking for basic facts, such as whether the school is a university or college, whether it is public or private, its religious affiliation, its undergraduate enrollment, its location, a list of majors, varsity sports, clubs and activities.

Using these websites will help you begin your college search, and by clicking on any of the colleges on the search results list, you can open the individual college's website. You should also consult your school counselor or independent college advisor for a potential college list or check out your Web-derived list with a college specialist.

Starting Out

Having found a list of potential colleges, start with each college's website. Although the college home pages differ from one another and no two sites are alike, they generally include common features that you may have to decode to uncover the real nuggets of information. Remember when viewing these sites that the college is putting its best foot forward, and just as an admission officer might look askance at an application with shoddy proofreading, you should critically appraise what you see. If the college has an obvious error on an important page, or if the website is years old and hasn't been updated, it is worth noting that this may poorly reflect on the college.

After first learning of the college through the College Search feature on collegeboard.org, Tim continued his search by typing "McCrea College" into a Google search. The top hit was the college's website and he clicked on it. Up came a beautiful picture of the campus, with banners in the college's team colors. There were rotating pictures and there were links to "About McCrea," "Academics," "Student Life," "Admission" and "Athletics." There were banners giving links for "Prospective Students," "Current Students," "Faculty/Staff," "Parents and Families" and "Alumni." There was a search bar, a site index, an alumni donation link and a hodgepodge of links of varying importance. There were articles on current students, a famous alumna and building plans. There were ways to connect to Facebook, Twitter, YouTube, Linked In, Delicious and Zinch. There was a letter from the president, a short sampling of recent news items about McCrea and a small picture of a campus map. And there were about a dozen other tabs and links for "Facts," "Departments and Majors," "Clubs & Organizations," "Civic Engagement," "Sustainability," "Apply," "Financial Aid & Tuition," "Arts," "Music & Theater" and "Visit Campus." Tim was confused and worried. He decided to look at another school and found the same basic structure and the same overwhelming patterns. How could he possibly figure out these sites and get the information he was interested in without spending hours on the computer?

Cassie, who wanted to know if there was a singing group at Calder College for people who weren't music majors, also wanted to know if the college had a good physical therapy or occupational therapy department. She went to the college's website and found lots of things to click on, but couldn't find the answers within a couple of clicks.

It turns out that Tim and Cassie were right: Many college websites are confusing and complicated. Even for students who have been attending the college, such a website is difficult to navigate and to use to discover the desired material. Nevertheless, there is much solid, factual information about the college that you can learn from patient viewing of its official Web page. Remember that large state universities may have more complicated websites because they must cover so many different areas, while small colleges might be easier to browse. Both reflect the makeup of the different kinds of colleges.

Because it's easy to get lost when surfing college websites, it's important to have a list of questions to guide your research. Look at Chapter 6, "Chief Aspects of College Life," and *use those questions of interest to you* as you browse a college website. Many of the answers to demographics, testing and application information questions are available through the college search websites. It is nevertheless worthwhile to compare the information from those sites because colleges usually present more updated information on their own websites.

The typical college website will have the following:

"Basic Facts" Tab

Basic facts about the college, often on an "About" link or a "Fast Facts" link, give the general overview of the college, with subsequent links that are usually easy to find.

- Name, address and history of the college

- Type of school and degrees offered: college or university

- Location of college: city, town or rural; population of the nearest city

- College enrollment

- Public or private; religious affiliation

- If a university, the colleges within

"Admission" Tab

This section includes essential facts about the application process.

- Academic requirements for admission

- SAT and ACT score range

- High school GPA of previous freshman class

- Application requirements, including transcript, recommendations, test scores; interview

- Deadlines for regular and early decision; early action

- Application fee

- Tuition and fees, room and board costs

- Financial aid percentage

- Scholarship information

- Link to the application itself

- Link to visit information

- Admission contact information

Some websites give you clues on what a college specifically looks for in an application, as the University of Michigan does. Some colleges, like Caltech, spell out exactly what they expect qualified applicants to have done prior to applying. Some, like Dickinson College, make it clear that you should contact the admission officer for your region, giving the names and email addresses of the person to contact, and sometimes the admission office even gives you a personal statement or Web page about that officer. If you find the name and email of a regional representative, you should, by all means, contact that person with questions and later send an acknowledgment note, as colleges look for demonstrated interest. (See Chapter 2, "What Colleges Look At.")

Jackson, a student from a single-parent household, found this practical information most useful on his website hunts, and he bookmarked those colleges that fit his considerations without going into the academic courses tab. Noah, on the other hand, found it far easier to lie in bed and survey the printed viewbooks that colleges had mailed to him after his initial email of inquiry. He had found it tedious to navigate from link to link, and on some sites got so lost that he felt he had wasted valuable time. He decided to check out College Prowler for each college and read what students were saying.

"Academics" Tab

When you search a university's website, it is often necessary to find the link to the college or school of interest, such as "Arts & Sciences," "Business," "Engineering," "Communications" etc., and then drill down to the departments and then to the majors within each department.

If you search in smaller liberal arts colleges or specialized colleges such as art schools or music conservatories, your task is more direct. Some schools require that you select your major when applying, and accept you directly into that major, which may have heightened requirements and more competitive admission than the school's general admission. Others have you apply for entry during freshman or sophomore year for your specific major. If you desire a specific major but can't immediately apply for admission into it, make sure you learn what the expectations are and what the chances are for getting into that major later.

It is not unusual for students to enter college with one major and then find they change their minds ... which is what college is all about: opening up novel ideas, different fields, new horizons. Don't pick a college solely for its major, but keep in mind other important aspects of college life. (See Chapter 6, "Chief Aspects of College Life.")

The "Academics" tab will often have:

- Majors and minors with links to departments and course offerings

- The average class size and the student/faculty ratio

- Required courses for college graduation

- AP/IB scores accepted for advanced standing and/or credit

- Faculty profiles

- Exchange programs

- Study abroad opportunities

- Academic calendar: semester, trimester, other

- Audition or portfolio requirements, if necessary

The "Academics" tab is particularly valuable, and neither Jackson nor Noah should have ignored this part of the website. Although each college differs in the extent that it details information about specific courses, most of them have a link to the individual professor teaching each course. Again, the faculty Web pages vary enormously, and you may find that many professors do not keep their pages up-to-date, but you will recognize a gem if there is a picture of the faculty member, an account of the professor's credentials with the degrees awarded from college and graduate schools, papers and books published, his or her interests and teaching philosophy and, most valuable, the professor's email address.

Mallory, a senior who wanted to investigate gender studies, was able to get a good tag on the colleges that had dynamic departments by scrolling through the women's studies courses and finding out what each professor emphasized on the faculty Web page. Emma, after her look at the website and then her campus visit, corresponded with the film professor at Burgess and learned more than the website had offered her. Remember, though, that not all faculty have the time to respond quickly, and some may not be keen on email correspondence.

"Costs/Financial Aid" Tab

Each college now posts an annual federally mandated "net-price" calculator on its website. The calculators are supposed to provide estimates of both the costs of the school and the expected financial aid package the student might receive. On the cost side, the colleges must show four areas of expenses: tuition and mandatory fees, housing and food, books and supplies, and transportation and personal expenses. The scholarships and grants side is broken down into school support, federal aid and state aid. But because these calculators are created and structured differently on each college site, and because many don't show the real-life costs, it may not be possible to compare colleges accurately.

As these calculators improve, they are potentially good tools for comparing costs and, to a lesser extent, comparing aid packages. You can use these calculators to see the "actual" costs of attending different schools, and then you may be able to determine if a school is priced out of your market or is close enough to other schools to make the cost difference irrelevant to enrollment decisions.

Any calculator will be only as good as the information entered. The college is obliged to reveal present costs, but if expected tuition and fee increases are not included, the picture given is not quite as transparent. Likewise, if some colleges expect that freshmen will eat 19 meals a week, while others will estimate only 14, the prices might not be comparable; or if a student wants a single or a double room, but receives a quad, the cost calculator will not reflect the real costs. The same is true on the financial aid side, where one college may give aid to students whose families earn less than $70,000, while another may give aid to families who earn less than $150,000. Some schools require loans while others award financial aid without students incurring loans.

Liz, for instance, saw that the costs of attending the private liberal arts college that she had her heart set on, after subtracting likely financial aid, were only marginally higher than her state university's costs. She also discovered that even though her state university's tuition was comparatively low, she hadn't thought about the mandatory fees, which were much greater than the tuition costs. It turns out that her state allows each university campus to keep its own fees, but forces the tuition dollars to go to the state treasury. Her state university used this anomaly to reverse the expected cost structure. She wouldn't have thought that had she only compared the tuition prices.

And even more importantly, some colleges offer generous merit scholarships to qualified students and some state universities offer substantial scholarships to out-of-state applicants, while some colleges nickel and dime extra expenses that are not included in the calculator. For instance, colleges may charge for tennis court usage while others charge for gym lockers; some colleges offer free laundry, while others have coin or debit-card operated washers and dryers; and some may provide a "free" computer or tablet, but the tuition and fees may be significantly higher than their competition. Some schools that have what appear to be high costs may actually charge less than expected because they freeze tuition at the freshman price, thus lowering the comparative upperclassmen rates. These subtle variations can have an impact that the college financial aid pages might not highlight.

"Athletics" Tab

Schools that are powerhouses in the major sports tend to have booster-type sites that show their athletic teams in action. These sites indicate:

- Importance of sports on the campus

- Number and type of varsity sports, with links to each sport

- NCAA division

- The name of the athletic conference to which the school belongs

- Roster of athletes in each sport

- Recruiting page for varsity sports

"Campus and Facilities" Tab

The ambiance on campus is indicated in a variety of visual ways, but it is extremely variable across different college websites. It is easy to be taken in by the very pretty pictures, usually posed and photographed on a bright day in spring or fall and to think that by clicking on the various links that you're experiencing the real thing. Just as a college may seem more attractive on a sunny, beautiful day or less inviting on a cold, rainy day, a college's website can present both an unclouded picture that can't reflect all the realities of life on campus, or a dim portrait of a campus that is actually quite clear to the students who attend. However, sometimes with different links, you'll find:

- Map of the campus and photo tour

- A view of important buildings: "Old Main" and other historic buildings, library, residence halls, dining halls, science and computer labs, fitness center and student center

- Health, counseling, career services

- Special-needs services

- Campus security

- Construction and renovation plans

- Residence halls and perhaps room layouts

Finding Hidden Information

Cassie discovered that students who looked at Calder College also looked at Whistler College, so she went to the Whistler College website and clicked on the "About Whistler" tab. She discovered that Whistler was located in a suburb of St. Louis, that it had 3,000 undergraduates pretty evenly split between males and females and she also saw pictures of a beautiful fall scene with lots of trees and old stone buildings. Her SAT score put her in the middle range listed and her grades were similar to those of accepted students. She noticed that the most popular majors were economics, political science and international studies. She went to the financial aid page and learned that two-thirds of the students received financial aid.

Whistler didn't have a separate tab for athletics, but she found it under a "Life at Whistler" tab. She saw that the varsity team played in Division III and that the football and women's basketball teams won the Missouri Intercollegiate Athletic Conference championship last year. Backing up to the "Life at Whistler" tab, she saw a list of over 50 clubs and student organizations, including two singing groups. By now, she was really interested in Whistler and wanted to know more about what it was like to go there. However, she found that many other details were harder to find.

Is My Major Available?

It's pretty easy to find biology or history or English majors, but if your interest isn't that straightforward, you might have difficulty finding it. As Cassie discovered on the Whistler College site, there was an "Academics" tab, which then led to a listing of majors, on which she clicked on the individual departments. Other fields are difficult to find, such as environmental studies, which might be listed under biology or ecology or an interdepartmental minor.

The only thing that Garrett knew about colleges was how well their teams played football and basketball. He only wanted to go to a school with winning teams, but he also realized that he had to think ahead toward a career. He determined that business combined with sports made a good combination and that would be how he would start his college search. Searching each college's "Academics" tab, he found that some business schools had a sports management major, but he also found that some sports management classes were embedded in human ecology schools, in others they were in tourism and hospitality and in still others they were in exercise science departments. In others there were only a few courses that related to his interest. Garrett had to figure out what all this meant.

Sometimes the best way to search for a particular major is to use the college website's search box, which limits the search to that college. Remember to try different names, spellings and abbreviations, as search engines cannot find terms that are not used at that school. Alexis, who wanted to study the literature of many countries, had to search "comparative literature," "world literatures," "global literature" and separate foreign language departments depending on the college she was researching. Cassie went to the "Academics" tab and saw that one of the majors listed was kinesiology, which she knew was another term for her interest in physical therapy.

What Is the Male/Female Ratio?

Many colleges avoid this topic ever since women became the majority of students enrolled in college. Some ratios are so skewed that the college website just doesn't give out this information. They don't want students to be turned off by an unbalanced ratio. However, if you can't find it, this statistic is available in books and in the College Navigator of the U.S. Department of Education website. You might also read the student newspaper for articles dealing with the ratio issue or ask this question directly on your campus visit.

What Are the Courses and the Faculty Really Like?

One of the most valuable parts of the website enumerates and details the academic departments and the courses. Pay particular attention to this vital, indispensable section. Skim through the departments and courses to see the range of offerings. Are there courses in studio art, art history, music, theater, dance, creative writing and film? Do the sciences include neuroscience and astronomy? What languages are taught? Are there women's studies or global diversity courses? What about anthropology or sociology? If you are interested in comparative religion, in what department are the courses? Are there accounting, engineering, computer science and education departments? Universities are more likely to have a wider distribution of specialties than small liberal arts colleges, but can you register for courses in schools within the university that are outside of your major? Each university has different rules, and if you can't find them on the website, you should ask in your interview or email an admission representative.

At the beginning of your search process, the following questions may be overwhelming, but when you are ready to make an intense review of your options, these questions, which go into depth concerning what the academics at each school are like, may help you make a decision about which college to attend.

Do specific departments, especially those in which you might be interested, show breadth and depth by the number of faculty, the number of courses offered and the range of subject matter? Does there seem to be a subspecialty in some departments, for example, a concentration of Russian or Slavic courses in the European history division or genetics in biology? Are there courses that deal with multicultural or multiethnic issues? Diego and Maria especially wanted to take courses in these areas.

Scan the requirements for a major in a department of interest. Are the required courses given annually, or are there some years when certain required courses are not offered? The latter might make for scheduling difficulties later on. For instance, if you choose to take your junior year abroad, would you have trouble finishing the required courses when you returned? Usually there are not specific descriptions of the courses, but can you get a clear idea of content? Are the instructors' names listed? Are there some courses that sound especially interesting?

Count the number of full-time faculty in your department of interest. Do a mere handful of instructors cover a large range of subjects? Because of scheduling, faculty members rarely teach more than two or three courses each semester, and it may mean that a course you desire won't be offered when you want it. Notice also if the professors teach from semester to semester and year to year, or if there are asterisks, daggers and slash marks scattered after their names. These symbols usually signal that the instructors will be away from classes during all or parts of the academic year and that certain courses may not be taught when these faculty are on leave.

The department faculty pages may include information about where and when they received their degrees. What colleges and universities did they attend? Do the institutions represent a specific section of the country or a mixture of geographical areas? Do you know if these universities are renowned in the professors' fields? Is there a preponderance of Ph.D.'s from one university? This might indicate a particular emphasis, specialty or bias in the department. Did a majority of faculty earn their degrees recently, which might mean they are young, or is there a mixture of degree dates, indicating a wide age range?

Compare departments within the college to see if a particular department has an especially large number of faculty members. This might indicate the relative importance of this department in the academic scheme. Is any department underrepresented by faculty numbers, and is this one in which you were hoping to major?

A large number of adjunct faculty members in certain departments such as drama or film might indicate specialists who come from the outside world to teach a distinct craft — theater makeup, for example; in other departments it may indicate a policy of hiring part-time instructors to keep costs down. Many colleges hire part-time faculty to avoid paying the higher salaries of full-time professors. In some cases, part-time teachers may not have the same dedication to students as full-time faculty, nor be as well integrated into the college's life. Their commitment to the college may not include office hours when they would be available for student conferences, although emails can often substitute.

Your careful viewing of the "Academics" portion of the website will add significantly to your knowledge of the college. Jot down your own questions as you read and take your list on your campus visit. As a result of your review of this material, you will be thoroughly prepared to query students, faculty and your admission interviewer. (See Chapter 17, "Questions to Ask Your Interviewer.")

What Happens to the Campus on Weekends?

Even though this is a topic of great interest to applicants, most college websites omit detailing what happens on the campus during the weekend. An actual visit, including conversations with current students, is probably the best way to find out, but it may be possible to learn something about the weekend activities from social media sites or the student newspaper. (See Chapter 9, "Virtual Visits and Other Ways to 'See' a College.") If you're trying to find out something from the college's website, look at the percentage of students who live on campus. Make note, though, that many students not counted as campus residents, especially in urban areas, live close enough to campus so that they shouldn't be considered commuters.

Are There Music, Singing or Drama Groups for Nonmajors?

Cassie tried to find this out. Most student organizations are listed in some manner within the "Student Life" tab on a college's website. But some colleges don't even have this link on their website, which can make it more difficult. And many colleges have the student activities groups listed under "Clubs" or "Student Organizations" without proper descriptions. "LowKeys," for example, turns out to be an a capella group, but Cassie didn't find this out until she found some YouTube videos of the group.

How Does Campus Diversity Affect Student Life?

Some schools list the percentage of students from different racial and ethnic groups, and the percentage of international students. Sometimes the numbers can hide the fact that students are separated into cliques and not mixing with each other. One way to decode this is to look at the people in the campus photos, especially those in the background or those in unstaged interaction. Although photos of students of color don't necessarily represent the actual diversity on a campus, these photos may represent the desired goals of the college in its effort to attract a more diverse student body. Students of color are often featured in the foreground, so an absence might be a significant signal about the lack of diversity. Look at the crowds in the background of an athletic event or in the dining hall and see if you can glean the social interaction from those pictures. You can also look at the photographs and listings of the faculty to see whether departments have minority faculty.

Carlos wanted to see if Hispanics were integrated into the Abbott College activities so he studied the pictures and counted the people who looked like him. He was disappointed to find only three pictures that fit his criteria, and decided he would research this further on College Confidential.

Anand, who wanted to study digital gaming, had to check several subject majors before finding courses at Thoreau University. He looked through the faculty pages and found that there were several scholars with Indian names. He decided to email one of the engineering professors to learn about diversity on campus.

Look at the campus newspaper, which usually has a link from the student life or campus media page or college newspaper's website. Check to see if students with ethnic names are writing for the paper, or whether issues affecting minorities are explored in the pages. There might be student blogs that cover these topics as well. Recently there was a controversy about Asian students on a California campus that exploded on YouTube. Check out these social media sites to get some insight into minority issues; browse the local newspapers to see what they say about what's going on at the campus and in town.

Look at one of the minor sports teams, such as baseball or softball, and see what the rosters show about minority representation. Or look at the list of famous alumni and see if it includes minorities and when they graduated.

Where Do the Students Come From?

Carlos wondered if there were students from his area at Abbott College and looked in the "Admission" section with its geographic breakdown and in "Athletics" with its varsity rosters that showed where the athletes are from. Varsity sports teams usually list their rosters, so finding out where the student athletes are from is pretty easy. Less popular sports, drama and singing groups and most clubs usually don't have rosters. Hampshire College, for instance, doesn't list its Ultimate Frisbee team, other than to have the names of the captains; Ithaca College lists the pieces the symphony plays and the soloists but gives no information about the individual members; fraternities might list the current president and famous alumni, as the University of Virginia does, but gives no roster of brothers; the University of Pennsylvania's Mask and Wig shows photos of the troupe but no identifying information. Some schools, like Occidental College, have student blogs that have information about the students, but most websites don't list that kind of information, possibly because it changes so often or it is considered private information. Carlos couldn't find his specific answer on the Web. He decided to email his question to the admission office. Still other ways to find this information is in the College Board Handbook or in data from the College Navigator in the U.S. Department of Education site, which describes every college and university in the United States and does break down the student enrollment into categories, including religion.

What Is It Really Like to Live on the Campus?

A typical college website shows campus living as a utopian garden. The students are happy; the students are busy cheering the sports teams or helping others; the school spirit is jumping out of the screen. How much truth there is you will have to discern for yourself when you visit. Lots of schools, though, have student blogs and you can get some insight into college life from them, and the social media sites highlight some aspects of college life. (See Chapter 9, "Virtual Visits and Other Ways to 'See' a College.")

Where Do the Students Study?

Again, the college's website will probably be inadequate for deciphering this question. A virtual trip to the library might show study carrels or you might catch a glimpse of how crowded the library is, and a listing under residential life might tell you if the floor lounges are used for studying.

When Does the College Have Breaks?

The academic calendar tells you when vacations and exams occur, and also whether the college runs on a semester, quarter, trimester plan, or variations known as 4-1-4 and block systems. Every calendar system has both advantages and disadvantages, which you can check out on your visit or question in your chats. The "Academics" site may tell you the calendar system the college is using.

What Special Programs Does the College Have?

Many websites include descriptions of special programs, tutorials or independent study, honors college, study abroad, interdepartmental programs, field study, internships or practicums or cooperative work-study. There are consortium affiliations such as the Great Lakes Associated Colleges and the Five Colleges in Pioneer Valley of Massachusetts, and combined degree programs of liberal arts and medicine like that at Brown, or a 3:2 program of liberal arts and engineering at Franklin and Marshall, or liberal arts and experiential learning at Allegheny. These programs overcome the confines of the campus and add breadth to the course of study.

Some unique programs include an artist- or writer-in-residence as Wesleyan boasts, or a special lecture series at Columbia. Some colleges have distinct freshman orientation plans such as Earlham's outdoor session, Bard's critical writing course, Ursinus's Common Intellectual Experience, or Kenyon's and Princeton's preparation programs for students of color. Many colleges have a freshman book project where every incoming student reads the same book and then discusses it with a variety of professors and outside speakers. Other colleges have theme-oriented freshman seminars and you choose one that interests you.

Look for the special programs at each college to see if there is something especially appealing to you.

Other Website Features

There are many other things that can be discovered that are important to both selecting the college that is right for you and for assisting you in targeting your application. For example, you can discover if the college has a special emphasis. Most deans of admission believe their college has special attributes and that there are certain types of students who will fit in best at their college.

Look at the website and see: Is the school championing itself as a place that teaches "scholarship in action," as Syracuse University does, or does it emphasize "how to learn for a lifetime," as Carleton College claims? Or is the school like Guilford College, "a place where questioning answers is valued as much as answering questions," or like Baylor that states it "will instruct you and teach you." Each school has a theme embedded in its website that gives you a clue to its mission and to what types of students the admission office is looking for.

Madeleine, as the daughter of a French mother and an American father, was fluent in two languages. Although her high school in France would give her an International Baccalaureate diploma (IB) that qualified her for college in most countries, Madeleine decided to attend an American college. She wanted a place where there was lots of diversity and a sophisticated, intellectual student body. She was looking for a college that focused on the works of great thinkers and emphasized intellectual learning. As she frequently visited her American grandparents, she began to visit those colleges whose mission was compatible with her interests, and then followed-up with an extensive look at their websites to narrow down her list before making in-depth visits.

The Mission Statement

Most college websites have a college mission statement; however, many students overlook this feature without realizing what a gem it can be. Sometimes the statement is part of the rotating pictures decorating the main page of the college; more often there is a specific area, often within the "About" or "Academics" tab where the key to understanding the educational mission is found. When you see statements that say the college's mission is "unique," "unusual," or "special" or tell you something about the college's emphasis, then you should read the text carefully and gauge whether it relates to you. Zack found this relevant when searching for colleges that emphasized civic involvement, Hao was interested in an international outlook, and Emma sought statements that encouraged creativity.

If a school places emphasis on international learning, or proclaims its "global experiences" or "interdisciplinary" perspective, or states that it has a "rigorous" or "structured" educational philosophy, or "uniquely" combines service learning, or is "unusually committed" to environmental responsibility, you should then gauge your interest against that of the college. Kayla found colleges that appealed to her strong global outlook by reading some mission statements.

New-Student Orientation

Most colleges conduct orientation sessions for freshmen before classes begin. Many have optional orientation programs including community service projects or outdoor activities — these are geared less toward academic orientation and more toward bonding and creating community. Some schools have summer orientation programs where students come to the campus for a few days in the early summer both to register for classes and to begin the process of acclimatizing to college. Other schools have a specific freshman orientation session that begins a few days before the upperclassmen return to campus.

These sessions are invaluable for the students attending them, but the orientation website entries that discuss them are also important tools in assessing what college life is really like on the campus, what the course and graduation requirements are, and what the college thinks is important enough to include in the first days the student is on campus. Look for the "Freshman Orientation" link for further information as this section often reveals actual activities, courses and requirements. Sometimes this is the only place where you will find this specific information.

Pros and Cons of College Websites

Jeff and Emma both knew that until they saw a college in action, they couldn't know what the students are really like, how good the instruction is, how intense the academics are, or how exciting learning is on any particular campus. But they could gather some solid information about the college on its website that is excellent preparation for their actual visit and a necessity if they can't make a campus trip.

✓ Pros and Cons of College Websites

Best Uses of a College Website

❏ Discover basic facts about each college.

❏ Find admission information.

❏ See tuition, financial aid and scholarship information.

❏ Get athletic information.

❏ Explore academic courses.

❏ Learn about professors.

❏ Get and use email addresses of professors.

❏ View layout, buildings and facilities.

❏ Read school newspaper.

❏ Find out about alumni.

❏ Chat with students about each college.

❏ Get a visceral feel of the college.

❏ Prepare for your visit.

❏ Get traveling directions.

❏ Learn about clubs and other student activities.

❏ Find student-produced videos, photos and blogs.

What's Not Always Good

❏ Detailed information on courses.

❏ Insight into the social aspects of college.

❏ Academic quality of faculty.

❏ Interaction among students.

❏ What the average student is like.

Viewer Take Care

❏ Every website is differently organized and takes time to navigate.

❏ A slow website is not necessarily a reflection of a college's quality.

❏ A fast, glossy site is not necessarily an indication of excellence.

❏ A college's website is designed to portray its strengths.

❏ Campus photos online show only the best weather and the happiest students.

Chapter 9

Virtual Visits and Other Ways to "See" a College

What Is a Virtual Visit?

Jim wanted to see what Thoreau University was like, but he couldn't take the long trip. He read an "insider's guide" report on Thoreau and he gleaned that the campus had the excitement he hoped for. He was pretty savvy browsing the Web and he figured that he could find some information sites and videos that would confirm what that report said. He started by searching for Thoreau. He immediately found the university website, but after a quick look, he moved to the next few entries. The first one carried him to a site that promised videos of Thoreau, but he only found links to online colleges there. Then he tried the next site and found a listing of college visit reports which seemed to be written by parents. He switched to a video search and he found lots of Thoreau videos, including a slickly produced one that featured the university's president, and another one that seemed to have been shot from a cell phone that showed students playing beer pong. He decided to go back to the college's website and start from there.

Jim discovered the world of the virtual visit: a cottage industry of video producers who make official college videos that compete on the Web with a cottage industry of amateurs creating YouTube videos for fun. There are unaffiliated websites like Campus Confidential designed to get students and parents to communicate with others about various colleges, and there are websites designed to steer students to particular colleges and often to for-profit institutions. Just as the Web can provide information about just about anything, sometimes the world of the virtual visit is a mass of official, unofficial, accurate and inaccurate information about colleges. The first words for anyone attempting a virtual visit to a college are: VIEWER BEWARE.

College Website Virtual Visits

Most colleges have some form of visit available on their websites. Sometimes these include pictures and descriptions of the important campus buildings, sometimes they are videos with student tour guides, and sometimes they are officially sanctioned videos with the college president and deans telling you about their college. Learning to browse and decode a college's website is an important part of the virtual visit, but it is only one of the many ways that you can make such a visit. If you want a quick overview of a college, the virtual visits produced by the school will give that to you. Some colleges have even begun to promote affiliated sites with updated blogs, videos and Twitter feeds produced by current students for prospective students.

Where to Go

You can make a virtual visit to almost every campus in the United States. Virtual visits are available through Facebook, YouTube, Flickr, Zinch, College Prowler, Campus Confidential, YouniversityTV, Campus Grotto, StudentAdvisor, Unigo and Wikipedia, and they can even be made without leaving your search engine. In fact, it is so easy to make these visits that you may be tempted to leave the driving until move-in day. While it is true that you can discover lots of information from these websites, it would be a mistake to believe that these virtual visits can be a realistic substitute for a feet-on-the-ground visit.

Virtual Visits as Advertising

Websites come and websites go. While you might think that a website is there solely because its information is important and useful, it is essential to remember that most websites are actually there to make money for the owners of the site. What was a useful site one day can later become simply a conduit for businesses to advertise to a market of teenagers. Be careful who and what you trust and make sure you spend more than a few moments on a website that shows what you want to see. Just because a review of Abbott College shows that all the students are "hot," or claims that Whistler College has the "most active" student political scene, doesn't mean that it's true. And remember that some sites are really pushing for-profit colleges in the guise of providing information about lots of other colleges.

Facebook Is Everywhere

Facebook has become the meeting place for this generation, and colleges have noticed. Most colleges have multiple Facebook pages, with separate pages for each school, each freshman class, and even most groups on campus. Some colleges have staff who follow the activities on the pages, create links to activities on campus and make comments on the postings, often curating the site to make sure information presented is accurate and editing passages that might be offensive. Other colleges have a laissez-faire attitude toward Facebook and have little to do with the content or even whether the content is up-to-date or accurate. And sometimes it is hard to tell which is which.

What we do know is that most students don't want colleges invading their own Facebook pages. College admission staff can, and sometimes do, research applicants by checking on Facebook entries, so if you have questionable items in yours, you should clean it up prior to submitting your application. (See Chapter 12, "Other Types of Interviews.")

Sometimes Facebook entries are deceiving. Cassie friended her cousin who was a freshman and very aware of the party scene at Abbott College. It seemed like parties began each week on Thursday and ended late on Sunday night. Cassie wondered how her cousin ever got work done, or whether going to classes was even a part of life at Abbott. She went to Campus Confidential and read the few entries there, most of which concerned high school students wondering if they could get in. Campus Prowler was a little more helpful, but Cassie was surprised to find that nightlife was rated a C-. She decided that she'd speak to her cousin on the phone and texted her to find a good time to talk. Her cousin told her that most of her friends at college used Facebook to show each other how much fun they could be and that her page didn't reflect what was really going on. She agreed with the Campus Prowler rating and said that Abbott students spent too much time studying and not enough having fun.

Viewbooks

Many colleges still print viewbooks. These booklets are generally produced by the publications office of the college or by a public relations team hired by the college to produce handsome reports. Like the college's website, these usually show everything at its pictorial best. You can, however, get a look into what the college is promoting — it could be the worthiness of their science labs or the variety of drama productions or both — and this probably means that these programs are well supported.

If college viewbooks are your chief source of academic information, scrutinize them especially carefully. Ask yourself what image the college is trying to project in its polished pictures. At some point in your college search, you must check to see if that image is a reality or a promotional come-on.

What are the students doing in the pictures — ambling about a sun-drenched campus, coeds arm in arm? What do you know about the actual weather in that part of the country or the male/female ratio? Are there pictures of students working in the library, studying a microscope slide, listening in class? Do the students all look the same? Is there an ethnic or racial mixture portrayed? Sparkling pictures may embody a recruiting technique and desire rather than reality. You must question what the college is trying to tell you about itself and its emphasis and you must try to find out how accurate the presentation is.

Other sources of information are special publications featuring a particular department or activity. If you email the college asking for information and state that you're interested in chemistry, Latin American studies or soccer, for example, you may receive a special brochure on that subject describing the courses, career possibilities or activity.

A Walk Through the College

Liz was busy with band practice and concerts and knew she wouldn't have time to travel to every campus that interested her. Many websites, including some college websites, have student-led tours of campuses. These can be a great introduction to a campus layout, the important buildings and the look of the students who attend. Some sites, notably College Week Live and Youniversitytv.com, have tours and discussions that are as good as some on-campus tours and information sessions. Walking through the campus online is a great way to assess a college and see if your gut reaction to the campus is positive or negative. Videos of regular collegiate tours taped by counselors are another walk-through, but these cost around $15 per college. If the tour is well produced, you might see more than on an actual tour, but you miss the opportunity for happenstance encounters with live students. Seeing students eating in a dining hall is really no substitute for being there yourself. But, through the virtual tours, Liz was able to narrow her choices down to a manageable number. (See Chapter 2, "Some College-Related Books and Websites.")

College Apps

Derek loved following sports on his iPhone and when it came time to look at colleges, he was comfortable browsing there for college information. With the proliferation of smartphones, colleges are increasingly marketing to the mobile consumer by creating campus apps. Some apps are designed to be cutting edge, looking and feeling more like video games than a traditional college website. The majority of apps generally link to parts of the campus website, and sometimes the apps are easier to navigate than going directly to that site. If you like viewing material on tablets and phones more than on a computer, then these apps are a good way to learn about a college. If not, the space available on a computer screen gives a better viewing experience and enables you to see more of the subtle material necessary for decoding the college website.

Other Sources

It can be amazing what you can discover simply by using a search engine and typing in the name of a college that interests you. There is always a Wikipedia entry that will tell you something about the history and famous alumni of the college. And there are increasing numbers of videos and blogs written by and for students and applicants.

Maria, who was going to be the first in her family to go to college, searched for Calder College and found a link to college application videos. Like a few other colleges, Calder allows students to supplement their written applications with an original video or other creative submission. She was mesmerized by the originality and talent of the applicants. While this show of creativity scared her a little at first, after watching a dozen of these videos, she had already come up with an idea of her own. She knew that Calder was moving toward the top of her list.

The Web is often the best place to look for information about colleges that are not well known. There are many college-related sites that cater to students who have little or no idea what college is all about, and sometimes you may gain insights or information that even current students might be unaware of. Remember when browsing these sites that accuracy is not always first and foremost and websites might focus on superficial features of the campus. Likewise, when reading student reviews or comments, note that each student is bringing his or her own perspective and idiosyncrasies to the page and a focus on a campus incident one year might be irrelevant to current student life a year later. Very often the writer is at one extreme of joy or the other extreme of disappointment — the moderates usually stay out of it. The more you know about the source of your information, the easier it is to assess whether the opinions stated are relevant to your own situation.

Put Your Questions Out There

There are numerous sites that allow people to ask questions and receive answers from current students, prospective students, parents and sometimes even college representatives. Although sometimes these sites can be highjacked by current or former students who have particular axes to grind, these social network sites often give you insight into a college that you otherwise might not obtain.

Well-known colleges have more threads and a greater number of active participants. Many students ask the group about their chances for admission given their particular attributes, including scores, grades and extra-curricular activities, but even if these informal opinions are based upon good insights, they are, of course, not necessarily accurate or binding on the admission office. Careful students, while respecting the opinions presented on the sites, still do their own research.

Taking Advantage of the Virtual Visit

As an introduction to a college, virtual visits can be quite useful. Part of selecting a college is getting a gut feeling about the campus and the students, and virtual visits can provide an *initial* gut check. Reading about famous alumni or watching a video tour of the campus can give you an impression of a school that might differ from what you previously thought. Jeff thought that Parkman University was dominated by fraternities, but when he saw videos of an honors political science class, he noted that not everyone looked preppy. Mallory thought Calder College might be the right place for her, but after reading in College Confidential about the struggles of gay students to fund a dance, Mallory decided that she needed to make a real visit to Calder to find out more about the LGBT student group.

Tyler didn't have Eames College on his list, but as he was browsing on Unigo he found Eames and read that every student raved about the school. He decided to check out its website, then he checked out photos on Flickr and then he watched some YouTube videos about the campus. Finally, he made a real visit. Eames rose to the top of his college choices.

Luke's family had done a ton of community service both locally with their church group and nationally after tornadoes in Tennessee and hurricanes in Texas. Luke wanted to attend a college that was sincerely engaged in service commitments with students who were actively involved. He surveyed websites, including one that listed the 20 colleges most committed to community service, and he then began a serious review of those schools. First he saw whether his grades and ACT scores were in the ballpark, and then he looked at the colleges' websites. After selecting the five that seemed best from that sifting, Luke then read online reviews and searched for videos of the colleges. He was now ready to make his actual campus visits and was prepared to ask questions at his interviews.

A well-known advertising slogan tells shoppers that "an educated consumer is our best customer." This is undoubtedly true for the college shopper. The more you learn about a college, both on and off the campus, the better you are able to determine if the college will fit you now and serve you well as you change and mature. The explosion of information on the Internet makes it much easier to learn essential information and hidden facts that can help you choose your college. But while it would be a mistake to skip the wealth of information available on the Web, it would also be a mistake to rely solely on what you learn online. The virtual visit should be a starting place, not a sole source, in forming your college list.

Pros and Cons of Virtual Visits

A virtual visit via a college website, other website or social media serves as a valuable introduction to the college. Because of its variability and the extent to which it depends on a creative site designer or videographer, a virtual visit cannot take the place of a reality-based, on-site visit. A college website cannot give you the soul and ambience of the campus. A video will not address the quality of the academics. You cannot taste the food on the Web or sit in the cafeteria and hear the buzz. Above all, you cannot talk face-to-face with students. In essence, a virtual visit cannot tell you whether or not you'll fit in.

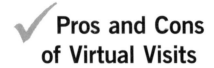

Pros and Cons of Virtual Visits

Pros

❏ You can make lots of visits without leaving your room

❏ Get a gut check to form your own opinion

❏ Discover insight into the social life

❏ Ask questions and get answers

❏ Help you prepare for a visit

❏ Find colleges to apply to

Cons

❏ Accuracy is questionable

❏ Opinions from anonymous people who have their own axes to grind

❏ A skewed view of the social life

❏ Sometimes TMI

❏ Advertisement disguised as information

❏ Admission office may learn more about you than you intended

Chapter 10

Your Campus Evaluation

Colleges are complex institutions. It really isn't possible to know everything about a college after a brief visit, and even students who have been there for several years might have a hard time giving you an accurate character reference for their college. But visits are the best way to gather clues about a college, especially if you investigate in a rational and systematic manner.

Many colleges may seem similar until you look more carefully at individual aspects. The "College Evaluation Checklist" will help you determine the character and distinctiveness of a specific college and be an aid in comparing colleges. In some parts of the list you may be checking more than one item. You can use the categories as a basis for discussion with your parents and friends. Make as many photocopies of the checklist as you need to cover all the colleges you will be visiting.

College Evaluation Checklist

College
Founded_____

Location_____

Enrollment:
Total undergrad _____ men _____ women_____

Visit
Date_____

Weather: ❏ sunny ❏ rainy ❏ gray ❏snowing ❏ other

In session _____

Costs
Tuition _____ Fees _____

Room and board _____

Books and supplies _____ Transportation _____

Type

❏ public   ❏ private   ❏ religious   ❏ 4 year

❏ 2 year   ❏ university   ❏ liberal arts   ❏ coed

❏ historically black ❏ technical   ❏ single sex

❏ Native American ❏ specialized   ❏ Hispanic serving

Architecture

❏ redbrick   ❏ gray stone   ❏ concrete block   ❏ Gothic

❏ colonial   ❏ classical   ❏ modern   ❏ mixture

Other _____

Calendar

❏ semester   ❏ quarter   ❏ trimester   ❏ 4-1-4

❏ block   ❏ summer session

Academics   ❏ liberal arts / sciences ❏ engineering ❏ business ❏ honors college
other _____

❏ pressured   ❏ moderately relaxed   ❏ stimulating
❏ bookish   ❏ dull   ❏ huge classes ❏ large classes
❏ small classes ❏ lectures   ❏ discussions
❏ tutorials   ❏ seminars   ❏ innovative
❏ traditional ❏ career oriented

❏ core curriculum   ❏ general ed   ❏ clusters
❏ required courses   ❏ distributive requirements
❏ requirements only in major   ❏ research opportunities
❏ language required   ❏ math   ❏ science
❏ senior thesis   ❏ capstone project
❏ strong departments   ❏ weak departments
❏ popular majors

Faculty   % Ph.D.'s _____   % part-time faculty _____
number of woman professors _____
number of minority professors _____
number of adjuncts _____

Popular Professors
❏ teach freshmen   ❏ teach upperclassmen
❏ teach what courses _____
_____
_____

Special Programs
❏ interdisciplinary   ❏ independent study   ❏ research
                                                opportunities
❏ study abroad   ❏ internships   ❏ consortium
❏ combined degree   ❏ cooperative programs ❏ double major
❏ unusual majors   ❏ honors program
❏ Phi Beta Kappa   ❏ freshman seminars
❏ freshman orientation   ❏ capstone experience

Students

❏ look-alikes ❏ diverse ❏ friendly ❏ interesting

❏ spirited ❏ smart ❏ preppy ❏ religious

❏ bizarre ❏ tattoos ❏ outdoorsy ❏ casual

❏ sloppy ❏ artsy ❏ outgoing ❏ preprofessional

❏ rah-rah ❏ intellectual ❏ grinds ❏ careerist

❏ geeks ❏ gamers ❏ loners ❏ jocks

❏ vegans ❏ liberal ❏ moderate ❏ conservative

❏ radical ❏ straight ❏ LGBT ❏ international

Other _____

Social Life

❏ college sponsored ❏ student initiated ❏ clubs ❏ sports oriented

❏ multicultural ❏ international ❏ fraternity ❏ sorority

❏ religious ❏ ethnic ❏ racial ❏ political

❏ wild parties ❏ mild parties ❏ dances ❏ dating

❏ group socializing ❏ drug and alcohol pressures

❏ leave campus on weekends

Problems _____

Housing

❏ dorms ❏ residential colleges ❏ apartments ❏ houses

❏ special interest ❏ fraternity ❏ sorority

❏ on campus ❏ off campus ❏ singles ❏ doubles

❏ suites ❏ coed ❏ single-sex ❏ transgender
❏ substance-free

❏ spacious ❏ adequate ❏ crowded ❏ rundown

❏ quiet ❏ noisy ❏ sociable ❏ disability access

Problems _____

Dining
- ❑ dining hall ❑ cafeteria ❑ residential college ❑ sociable
- ❑ food court ❑ snack bars ❑ coffeehouses ❑ bars
- ❑ special meals ❑ vegan ❑ kosher ❑ halal
- Quality: ❑ high ❑ adequate ❑ low
- Quantity: ❑ generous ❑ adequate ❑ meager
- ❑ open late hours

Recreation and Activities
- ❑ team sports ❑ intramurals ❑ gym ❑ playing fields
- ❑ fitness center ❑ athletic clubs ❑ student center
- ❑ music ❑ drama ❑ movies ❑ art museum
- ❑ newspapers ❑ radio station ❑ TV station ❑ game room
- ❑ minority clubs ❑ Latino ❑ Asian
- ❑ multicultural ❑ international ❑ religious clubs
- Special/other _____

Services
- ❑ health ❑ counseling ❑ career ❑ employment
- ❑ tutoring ❑ special student ❑ computer ❑ internships
- ❑ bookstore ❑ security ❑ special needs
- Other _____

Library
- ❑ outstanding ❑ good ❑ adequate ❑ poor
- ❑ long hours ❑ weekend hours ❑ open stacks
- ❑ closed stacks ❑ lounge ❑ computer facilities
- ❑ good lighting ❑ spacious seating ❑ special collections
- ❑ departmental ❑ sufficient staff ❑ coffee kiosk

Off-Campus Community
- ❑ far ❑ near ❑ easy access
- ❑ city ❑ town ❑ suburb ❑ rural
- ❑ restaurants ❑ bars ❑ pizza ❑ mall
- ❑ movies ❑ shopping ❑ dancing ❑ music
- ❑ theater ❑ bookstores ❑ jobs ❑ internships
- ❑ cooperation ❑ conflicts
- Other _____

Rating

things liked most _____

_____

_____

things liked least _____

_____

_____

Overall Rating

❑ superior   ❑ good   ❑ adequate   ❑ disappointing

Other

_____

_____

_____

_____

_____

_____

_____

_____

Part 2
The Interview

Chapter 11

Putting the Personal Interview in Perspective

Student Concerns About the Interview

Maggie's hands were shaking as she approached the admission counselor. She didn't like the idea of talking about herself to a complete stranger. Ken's palms were sweaty as he anticipated the third degree. And Olivia, who had pitched in any number of softball games without a twinge of nerves, had butterflies in her stomach. These students were suffering from symptoms of that curable disease, interviewitis.

For many, the interview is the most intimidating part of the whole admission process. Some students are shy, some are afraid of boasting, some are nervous about not knowing the answers to a barrage of questions. Others think they have to entertain the interviewer with jokes and stories so they won't be asked about their academic record.

One reason for interview anxiety is that most students are not accustomed to talking about themselves, and just the thought makes them uncomfortable. Although you might have a definite idea about yourself, you may not have taken the time to organize your thoughts into a self-portrait. But if you develop a self-concept as part of your interview preparation, and understand what an interview is all about, you will find your interview jitters fading away. And after a few practice interviews you might even grow to like it. (See Chapter 13, "Putting Your Best Foot Forward.")

What Is the Personal Interview?

The personal interview is a *conversation* lasting anywhere from 30 minutes to an hour between two people who share a common purpose. Simply put, it is an *information exchange*. You want to tell the interviewer about yourself, and you want to hear about the college; the interviewer wants to hear about you and wants to tell you about the college. There is no pass or fail and it's not the third degree. It's not a rehashing of the transcript, a repeat of the application or a rerun of the college website. It is an interchange between two people attempting to explore new ground together.

Why Have an Interview?

One purpose of the interview is to *give yourself an extra boost*. This is your opportunity to show the admission counselor something interesting about you. All during the application process the admission staff learns about you from a slew of papers: your transcript, test scores and application form. While it is true that you may make a vivid impression in the personal essay and in the recommendations from your teachers and counselor, words on paper can reveal only part of you. In the interview you have the chance to represent yourself directly. Only once during the whole admission process do you appear as the real, live person you are. That time is in the personal interview.

The interview is your opportunity to talk at some length to an admission counselor to present a sense of the singular blend of qualities that are yours alone. It's a chance to be your own advocate by talking positively about your interests and enthusiasms.

Laurie, for example, was exuberant and lively. She studied art outside of school and volunteered in a hospice, and her excitement about her work clearly came across in person. Warren had informed opinions that he was eager to share on everything from rock music to nuclear disarmament. Kiyo was heavily committed to a complex science project, and Amanda's strength was her ability to work congenially with many different people. Joe was involved in an intricate business enterprise, and Keith was a good all-around athlete. They each took the opportunity at their interview to put a face, or portrait, on their written application and be remembered.

The interview is the time to explain a spotty transcript or discuss any extenuating circumstances that affected your studies. Problems that you may find hard to write about in the application are often easier to discuss with a sympathetic admission counselor. Devon, for instance, had never been a good math student, but this hadn't stopped him from taking advanced math classes. He wanted to tell the interviewer why he had persisted despite the difficulties. When Scott's parents divorced, his academic work took a downturn, and it showed on his record. Haley was dyslexic and needed to make an extra effort with every assignment. Kim's family had moved three times in the past seven years, and each time she had readjusted to a new school and new friends. The interview is a good time to discuss such special situations.

The personal interview will also help you discover the distinctive characteristics of the college not readily found on its website or easily learned from students on campus. The interviewer is qualified to discuss your concerns about the college and answer your queries. (See Chapter 6, "Chief Aspects of College Life," Chapter 8, "Surfing and Decoding a College Website" and Chapter 17, "Questions to Ask Your Interviewer.") You will gain more knowledge and a better understanding of the college community, which will help you recognize whether the college is right for you. In addition, having interviews now when you are a high school student will make future job interviews less intimidating.

How Important Is the Interview?

Many colleges do not require an interview and therefore do not weigh the interview in their admission decision; otherwise, they would be rewarding those students who have interviews and penalizing those who do not. At those colleges where the interview is required or recommended (usually small private colleges, highly selective colleges and nontraditional colleges), the interview is one of many factors in the admission decision and is becoming a more important part of the application process.

Some colleges are foregoing the personal on-campus interview as they have decided it is not "cost effective," deeming that admission staff time is better spent on the active recruitment of applicants. These colleges send admission representatives to many high schools across the country to talk to students in their own settings. Other colleges send reps to different regions and they schedule interviews in hotel meeting rooms for students from the area. For students, it is an opportunity to ask questions and to speak briefly to these reps. Others conduct interviews via Skype or Facetime. (See Chapter 12, "Other Types of Interviews.")

Typically, interview notes are placed in the applicant's file, and the admission committee reads them last. The notes are used to confirm all the other material. "If there is a discrepancy between a teacher recommendation and the interviewer's perception," said one admission counselor, "we go with the teacher's report. We figure that the teacher knows the candidate much better than we do in our half hour with him."

The Admission Counselor's View

Although many admission counselors like students to interview at their college, they acknowledge that the personal interview is not essential, nor is it a key factor in admission decisions. There is widespread agreement among admission counselors, however, that a personal interview can work in a student's favor by putting a face on the written application. One admission counselor explains that the interview can personalize the whole application: "The interview is the occasion for a student to say something pleasant about herself, to confirm the academic record, and to explain something in the record that needs interpretation. The interview can make a difference if you let us know more about you. It's a chance to toot your horn."

All admission officers agree that the "borderline student," the student who is in the "gray area," is most likely to benefit from the one-to-one contact of the interview, especially if the student is willing to speak meaningfully about him- or herself.

Admission counselors also report that they do not use the interview to weed people out, but to keep people in the running. According to one counselor: "This is no time to be modest. If a candidate mumbles only 'Yes' or 'No' and doesn't make an effort to have some input, then the interview is probably a bust and isn't going to help." If you think you might be a "Yes–No" candidate, read Chapter 15, "Tips for the Shy Person."

Interviewers want to see *the genuine you.*

The Student's View

From your standpoint, the interview is very important. You should take every opportunity to give yourself a boost and enhance your written application by presenting your special qualities.

In addition, as a college shopper, you are looking the college over to see if it is a good match for you. The interview can sharpen your focus by illuminating the character and special qualities of the college. You can use the interview to ask questions about the college and to inform yourself of factors not covered in any other place. To discover if a college is one you should apply to, questions are the order of the day, and the interview is one opportunity to get the answers.

More from the Admission Counselor's Desk

The admission counselor has two purposes in the interview: First, to get to know you better; second, to get you to know the college better. Most interviewers are skilled at getting students to relax, which makes the meeting easier. They want the interview to be *a conversation, not a rehearsed speech.*

Counselors do admit, however, that their best conversations have been with students who come prepared, "students who know something about the college and are ready to talk." As one counselor said, "Don't blow it by asking, 'How many students are there here?' or, 'Do you have an English major?' or, as one student asked, 'Say, what college is this?' The well-informed, articulate person can really give herself a lift with a personal interview."

But the admission officer also knows that you are still a teenager and doesn't expect you to have fully formed goals, ideals and accomplishments. In wanting to know you better, the interviewer is looking for reasons to accept you, and your job is to provide them. (See Chapter 13, "Putting Your Best Foot Forward" and Chapter 14, "Planning for the Interview.")

To get you to know the college better, the admission counselor will talk about the college's strengths (and, if you push a little, the weaknesses). Most admission people regard the interview as a chance to give the candidate their personal view of the college, although they may differ somewhat on what this means. "The real value of the interview," says one admission counselor, "is that the student can try the college on for size, and the counselor can do good public relations for the college." But another counselor felt less strongly about the promotional aspect: "My role is as an advisor, not a salesperson. I want to tell the student about the college and help him or her make an honest decision."

When the admission counselor answers your questions and tells you about the college, listen. Give the interviewer your full attention. Don't jump from one question to another without waiting to hear the response. Nothing turns off an interviewer quite as much as the student who is merely showing off and only asking questions for effect.

Sometimes the interviewer will counsel you. If there are indications during the conversation that the college will not work in your best interest, the counselor may suggest other colleges that would. On the other hand, even though admission counselors do not ordinarily push their college, a counselor who sees you as a strong candidate may try to impress you with the college's numerous merits to convince you to apply.

Chapter 12

Other Types of Interviews

The Student Interview

In addition to the interview with an admission counselor, some colleges have their own students conduct the personal interview. These students don't usually sit in on the admission discussions, but their interview notes are filed in your application folder. You may find it easier to talk with a student, but your objectives should remain the same no matter who does the interviewing. (See Chapter 13, "Putting Your Best Foot Forward.")

The Alumni Interview

Still another kind of personal interview is with an alumnus or alumna of the college who lives in your area. You should take advantage of the alumni interview whenever it is offered, even if you've had an on-campus interview. The more people you talk to about the college, the better off you are. You will know more about the college and more people will know about you. The alumni interview is often arranged by the college after you have applied, and is always held in a public place, such as the interviewer's office, a coffeehouse or mall restaurant; the interview usually lasts 30 minutes to an hour. Alumni are customarily selected by the college and briefed on interview procedures. The interviewer may be an older, more traditional graduate or a recent graduate closer in age to you. Many colleges value the input of the alum interviewer, who is one more person who has seen you "up close."

The alumni interviewer knows only the basic facts about you: your name, address, ZIP code, phone number and high school. As a rule, alumni don't have your grades, scores or résumé. Their purpose is to have an exchange in which they learn about you and you learn about the college. They are evaluating you solely on the conversation. A common opening question is, "Tell me about your high school." They will often ask, "Why are you interested in my college?" and "What would you like to know about my college?" You have to be ready to speak about yourself, know lots about the college and be interested in what the alum says about the school. In other words, prepare for this interview just as you would for an on-campus one. After the interview, the alum sends a written evaluation to the admission office, often including a rating scale. It is always courteous to send a thank-you note or email to the alum after the meeting.

Group Interviews

Another type of interview is the on-campus informational group session. Colleges are turning to this, finding it a better use of staff time. Parents and students are invited to meet with an admission staff member in small groups, usually after a campus tour. The counselor talks about the college, sometimes illustrating his or her account with a video presentation, and then asks for questions from the group. This is a good time for you to speak up, and you can learn from listening to others' queries about things that may not have occurred to you. Because this type of interview is for information only, and is nonevaluative and nonjudgmental, you may find it less intimidating. Parents may find this a grand opportunity to ask questions. (See the Afterword, "For Parents.")

Group sessions are also utilized when the college representative, most often an admission counselor who covers your geographical area, visits your locality or your high school. Take advantage of this opportunity to hear about the college and make inquiries. After the session, introduce yourself to the representative and mention that you are planning to visit or that you already have. Show interest, but don't monopolize the person and prevent other students from talking.

Phone or Online Interviews

An admission person or alum may call you to answer questions or just to chat. Be relaxed, but if it is an inconvenient time or you are not prepared, ask the person to call again on a specific date and hour. Do a little homework and you'll be ready.

If you cannot come to campus, an admission counselor might suggest an interview via Skype or Facetime at a prearranged time. This is the closest thing to an in-person interview and should be accorded all the same preparation. Before going on camera, make sure you are properly dressed and that the background presents a pleasing, nondistracting scene as this is your face-to-face interview.

Special Note Re: Facebook

Although it's not actually an interview, a growing trend in admission offices is to check applicants on Facebook. They may just want to find out a little bit more about you to get some insight into your activities or to check out scholarship applicants' endeavors or just to get a broader view of their applicants. Students have pretty clearly stated that they don't want colleges peering into their lives, but if you're out there, the colleges can see you. It's a good idea, if you want to retain some confidentiality, to use the privacy settings. Better yet, employ the Grandma Test: If you think you would be embarrassed if your grandmother saw certain Facebook items of yours, scrub your page clean.

The Audition and Portfolio

Music conservatories, drama schools and dance departments hold auditions rather than interviews to evaluate candidates. The auditions are held on specific dates at the college or in centrally located cities around the country. It is best to know well in advance when you will audition and what is expected. You may be asked by the music school to perform several types of music representing different styles and periods, by the drama school to present several memorized selections and by the dance department to demonstrate your technique in a dance class. You should rehearse your pieces with your teacher or group well before staging the real thing. Liz didn't need auditions as she wasn't going to major in music, but Vanessa did. She played the clarinet and was interested in both jazz and classical music programs at music conservatories.

Art schools have their own version of an audition — the portfolio. Each art school has special requirements, so check with each one well ahead of time to make sure you have appropriate material. In addition, many art departments and specialized colleges participate in a "Portfolio Day" in large cities at which you can show your portfolio to a number of representatives and get their comments firsthand. This is a good thing to do in your junior year as many art representatives will give you advice on what you need to do to create a better portfolio.

Auditions and portfolios are different from interviews in that they are usually required and play an important role in the admission decision.

Special-Interest Interviews

The type of interview you have, and whom you interview with, might depend upon a particular interest you have in the college.

Athletes

If you are an athlete and want to play on a college team, talk to the coach in your sport. Arrange this ahead of time, before the beginning of your senior year, with the admission secretary or the athletic department, and bring along your scrapbook, statistics, video or other pertinent information that will help the coach learn about your talents. Understand and follow the NCAA rules and regulations. Your high school coach may have already made contact with several college coaches, but if not, you will want your coach to send a letter in advance. In any case, you can ask the college coach about your chances of making the team. You should also try to watch the team practice or compete to get an idea of its caliber and spirit.

Specific Interests

If you are interested in a particular field of study and want to find out more about it, speak to students who are majoring in that subject and make an appointment with a faculty member in the department. There is no better way to find out about the specifics of a department than to talk with the people directly involved. You can stay in touch with faculty by using their email addresses.

Carlos, who had founded and edited a high school psychology blog, emailed professors on his list of colleges to "talk" to them about their research projects and how his interests might fit in. He established such good relationships via email that when he visited and interviewed, he was warmly received. At one university, the professor recommended him for a special scholarship, which he applied for and received.

If you are interested in any extracurricular activity such as the newspaper, orchestra, radio station, intramural sports, or cheerleading try to speak to participating students. You'll find out what the activities are like and what your chances are of getting involved.

Ryan appeared at the radio station of Burgess College and the student staff member there interviewed him about his interests. Ryan spoke about his passion for modern American classical music, and without hesitation the student whipped out the staff appointment book for next year and said, "You'll have the 2 to 3 p.m. slot on Wednesdays to do your show."

You can use the checklist on the next page to keep track of your college interviews. Make enough copies of the blank checklist to cover all your interviews.

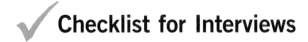 # Checklist for Interviews

College Name _____

Type of Interview
❏ personal ❏ group ❏ phone ❏ online ❏ athletic ❏ audition ❏ portfolio review

Date: _____ Time: _____

Name/Title of Interviewer(s): _____
_____
_____

❏ College representative ❏ alumni ❏ student ❏ coach ❏ faculty member
Contact/logon info: _____

Meeting Place: _____
Directions: _____
_____
_____
_____

Requirements: _____
Follow-up: _____
_____

❏ **Thank-you note sent**
Comments: _____
_____
_____
_____

Chapter 13

Putting Your Best Foot Forward

Your Mental Approach

Interviewing skills are not something you are born with, but are something you can learn. For starters, put aside the notion that the interview is an interrogation where you'll be bombarded with questions. Think of it as an exchange between two people learning about each other. And don't think the interviewer is looking for a certain type — he or she wants to talk to a real person, YOU. You don't have to pose, fake it or be someone you're not. BE YOURSELF. The golden rule for interviewing is: Know thyself and to thine own self be true. That's what it's all about.

Know Thyself

Usually, you are visiting colleges and having interviews before you apply, so the interviewer doesn't have a folder on you, and therefore knows nothing about you until you speak up. Sometimes you may be asked to fill out a brief questionnaire with your name, high school and course schedule, but generally the counselor doesn't know anything about you when you walk into the room. Your assignment is to put your best foot forward and to familiarize the interviewer with your distinctive personality. To do that, you must know yourself.

One reason for interview anxiety is that you may not be accustomed to thinking about yourself in an organized, lucid manner. If you're asked a personal question that you haven't thought about before, you might be surprised and thrown off base. The better you understand yourself beforehand, the more likely it is that you'll be confident dealing with anything that comes up. Effort spent getting to know yourself on your own time will pay big dividends. You won't be caught unaware if you do your soul-searching before the first interview. Here's how to begin:

- Analyze your personality

- Consider your strengths and weaknesses

- Assess your academic experience

- Evaluate your outside interests and activities

- Examine your values and goals

- Clarify what's important to you

Soul-searching requires time and patience, and should always be part of the college process whether or not you interview. We all have impressions about ourselves, but we seldom take the time to organize what we know into a "self-portrait." Keep in mind that you must be fair to yourself in your exploration. Don't underrate or exaggerate, and don't be so hard on yourself that your portrait is unrecognizable to those who know you well. Get feedback from your parents, friends and teachers to gauge if you're on the right track.

There are a number of ways to figure out your personal traits and qualities. Start with some words you might use to describe yourself. The "Know Thyself Vocabulary" on the next page provides an array of adjectives patterned after a list in a version of the *Georgetown University Law Center Career Handbook*. Check off all the words that apply to you, add ones that aren't included, and explore the pattern that emerges.

These descriptive words about you may also be used by teachers in their recommendations on your behalf. Show this check-off list to your teachers when you ask for recommendations and see if they agree.

Know Thyself Vocabulary

❑ reliable	❑ strong minded	❑ outgoing
❑ sociable	❑ cheerful	❑ eager
❑ enthusiastic	❑ ambitious	❑ determined
❑ bookish	❑ reflective	❑ cooperative
❑ relaxed	❑ daring	❑ curious
❑ understanding	❑ articulate	❑ lively
❑ calm	❑ optimistic	❑ idealistic
❑ hardworking	❑ resourceful	❑ motivated
❑ confident	❑ supportive	❑ supportive
❑ friendly	❑ progressive	❑ sincere
❑ fun loving	❑ bold	❑ conscientious
❑ analytical	❑ sensitive	❑ persevering
❑ loyal	❑ creative	❑ stable
❑ spontaneous	❑ patient	❑ alert
❑ original	❑ adaptable	❑ assertive
❑ modest	❑ adventurous	❑ broadminded
❑ practical	❑ strong	❑ serious
❑ tenacious	❑ careful	❑ thorough
❑ helpful	❑ natural	❑ logical

❏ imaginative	❏ thoughtful	❏ honest
❏ forceful	❏ considerate	❏ polite
❏ rational	❏ trustworthy	❏ poised
❏ fair minded	❏ independent	❏ empathetic
❏ realistic	❏ generous	❏ conservative
❏ private	❏ good natured	❏ warm
❏ liberal	❏ entrepreneurial	❏ individualistic
❏ introspective	❏ frank	❏ academic
❏ courageous	❏ organized	❏ energetic
❏ deliberate	❏ sensible	❏ flexible
❏ quiet	❏ consistent	❏ funny
❏ formal	❏ inventive	❏ persuasive
❏ easygoing	❏ intellectual	❏ responsible
❏ active	❏ tactful	❏ purposeful
❏ sharp	❏ mature	❏ competitive
❏ versatile	❏ successful	❏ firm
❏ happy	❏ capable	❏ clearheaded
❏ tolerant	❏ clever	❏ agreeable
❏ attentive	❏ quick	❏ industrious

❏ Other _____

_____

Your Academic Self

Other facets of the real you are your academic background and interests. Be able to describe your high school to someone who isn't familiar with it. Is the student body diverse or homogeneous? Do students and teachers respect learning and academic success? What is the quality of the teaching? Have any teachers inspired you and added to your school experience? Have they helped you develop your talents and interests? Do you think your school has prepared you for college study or are there areas in which you feel weak? Do you think your school has limited you in any way? How competitive is the atmosphere? Think of a sentence or two that describes your high school.

Consider the subjects you've enjoyed. Are there any areas of special interest to you? Have you written any papers or been involved in any important projects? Have any of these led to further interests in or out of school? Emma, for example, became interested in prison reform because of a paper she wrote on women in prison. Doug began writing poetry after reading Walt Whitman. Shawn's project on Martin Luther King Jr., stimulated his interest in African American history. Perhaps a paper you wrote had a similar effect on you.

Reflect on your academic program. What are your strongest subjects? Have you explored any subject in depth? Have you researched a topic that interested you? Has there been a course that was difficult for you? How did you handle it? Were there any special factors that made it difficult? Perhaps there have been external circumstances that interfered with your academic performance like parents' divorce, dyslexia or frequent family moves. (See "Dealing with Special Problems and Circumstances" in this chapter.)

Determine if your grades are a true estimate of your ability and potential. How do you feel about schoolwork? Are you taking honors, tough AP, or demanding IB classes or are you happier enrolled in regular courses? Have you done just enough to get by? Have you ever been challenged to work harder than you thought possible? Have you ever gone beyond the required assignments? Would you say you are an above-average, average, or below-average student? By defining your performance, purpose and interest in school, you'll get a good idea of your academic self.

The Nonacademic You

Another dimension of your personality is revealed through the activities you've been engaged in after school and during the summer. Where have you put most of your energies and talents? What activities have meant the most to you? Have you contributed to your school or your community? Have you had an after-school job? How have you spent your summer vacations? Have you attained any leadership position, or won any awards? What have you gained from your community service hours? Do your activities demonstrate your competence, talent or commitment?

For example, Liz was involved with the school and county bands, and Steve taught himself the guitar. Mike was in any organization that had soccer in its name, and Rob was completing an Eagle Scout merit badge. Luke spent two afternoons a week at a soup kitchen, and Julia was a sprinter on the track team. Roger marched in the drum and bugle corps; Winona marched for Native American rights. Jeff perfected his tennis game, Doug his poetry; Kunio worked for a pizza place, Lucy for SADD (Students Against Drunk Drivers). Jim led the student government; Scott delivered newspapers; Diego was an after-school sitter for young twins who lived in his neighborhood. While Mandy endured the rigors of Outward Bound, Keith biked all over the countryside. Any activities like these that you've engaged in are an important part of your nonacademic self.

Use the "Checklist of Activities" to indicate the activities in which you've been involved.

Checklist of Activities

❏ Academic honor society

❏ Art
  ❏ ceramics
  ❏ fashion
  ❏ film
  ❏ photography
  ❏ studio
  ❏ other _____

❏ Athletics _____(sport)
  ❏ intramural
  ❏ community
  ❏ recreation
  ❏ j.v.
  ❏ varsity

❏ Math or computer activity

❏ Music
  ❏ instrumental
  ❏ vocal

❏ Outdoor interests

❏ Political activity

❏ Religious activity

❏ Science activity

❏ School-spirit activity

❏ Student government

❏ T.V., radio or blog

❏ Volunteer work

❏ Jobs

❏ Clubs

❏ Civic affairs _____

❏ Community service _____

❏ Dance _____

❏ Drama or theater _____

❏ Ethnic or cross-cultural activity _____

❏ Environmental or green activity _____

❏ Foreign exchange or study abroad _____

❏ Foreign-language activity _____

❏ Journalism/Literary activity _____

❏ Leadership roles _____

❏ Other activities _____

Other Considerations

To talk about yourself in a meaningful way and project the real you, be aware of the goals and values that reflect your personality. Mandy cherished closeness with her friends; Rob steered his life according to the Boy Scouts' tenets and Liz expressed herself through her music. Luke's life was enriched by helping others; Karen's religion gave her strength; Rachel believed honesty counted most and Diego expected to serve his community. Do you have a star you steer by? What is it you care about?

Think about what you want to accomplish in the years ahead and how you would like to grow. Have there been any significant people, events or experiences that have shaped your development or your way of thinking? Be ready to talk about such meaningful experiences in your life.

Sometimes it is easier to think about yourself with a list of questions in mind. Some of the following have been used by interviewers to learn more about applicants. Mull them over to get a clear idea of who you are, what makes you tick, what you've been doing and where you're headed.

Twenty Questions

1. What three adjectives would your best friend use to describe you?
2. What have you enjoyed most about your high school years?
3. How have you grown or changed?
4. What activities have you found most satisfying?
5. What things do you do well? What are your talents?
6. What strengths would you most like to develop?
7. Have any of your courses challenged you? Which ones? How?
8. What achievements have given you satisfaction?
9. How do you respond to academic pressure or competition?
10. What would you change about your school if you had the chance?
11. What do you do for relaxation? For fun?
12. How do you define success?
13. How would you describe your family? Your community?
14. What do you want to accomplish in the years ahead?
15. What issues concern you?

16.   Is there any book, video or creative work that has had an impact on you?

17.   Is there an author, activity or field you've explored in depth?

18.   Have you had any stimulating intellectual experiences recently?

19.   How do you spend your summers?

20.   If you had a year to do anything you wanted, what would you do?

Agenda: Letting the Real You Shine Through

Now that you have started thinking about yourself, determine which aspects are important. Ask yourself what specific points you want the interviewer to know. What important matters do you want to impart to the interviewer *before* the interview is over? Make a list of several ideas that you want to discuss, and develop a concept of yourself that you want to get across.

A good idea for doing this is to think in three categories:

1.   Your academic interests and how they got started; what you've achieved, read, written or investigated

2.   Your extracurricular activities and how they have shaped you

3.   How you spend your summers, your personal interests and hobbies or jobs you've had and why any of these have been meaningful to you

Pick out *two* strong points in each category that are important to you and show your best features or your growth or strengths. Write these down. This is your Agenda, and when you are asked questions think how you can use your Agenda to answer the questions and let the interviewer learn significant things about you. By having an Agenda, you can gain some control over what otherwise might be a mysterious situation.

Think through how you would project this special blend of qualities to the interviewer. You don't want to puff yourself up by boasting about your assets, and you don't want to hide the real you by mumbling or whispering. You don't have to be a comedian, a hotshot, or a study in seriousness, and you don't want to be arrogant or self-important. You do want to be *honest, upfront*, and *positive*. You want to express your good qualities, activities and interests, highlighting your involvement and your personality. *Figure out how to be your own advocate.*

It is a good idea to talk about any strong interest developed over time, but it's not enough just to say you've been involved. You have to be able to discuss that activity's meaning for you. If you've been a ballet dancer since age seven, reflect on why you've stuck with it despite its hardships. If your main interest has been running track, be prepared to talk about your reasons for participating in it and the satisfactions you've had. If you've been in every show your school's put on, discuss the importance of those shows in your life, and how you enjoyed the cooperative effort. If you've worked in the student store, be able to say what it taught you about yourself and working with others. If you've been practicing to be a Super Bowl announcer, or to be first violin in a symphony orchestra, account for your interest and experience.

Whether you've been a joiner or a loner, a musician or a bookworm, a tinkerer or a scientist, a leader or a follower, a cheerleader or a biker, plan to talk about yourself with insight and discernment. Demonstrate that you've thought about yourself. Express your own point of view and your own spirit.

Treat the interview as an opportunity to discuss the importance of your activities, what gives them meaning. In an issue of *Glamour* magazine, an admission dean said, "Your goal is to show yourself at your strongest. If you talk about things that really matter to you, not what you think ought to matter, then you'll have a good interview." Mike realized that his soccer experiences had given him insights into his competitiveness; Lucy became a SADD activist to cope with the death of a classmate; Margo's cheerleading awakened her to the value of cooperation and teamwork. They all told their interviewers about these experiences as a way of communicating what mattered to them, and you should do the same.

Dealing with Special Problems and Circumstances

Most students have experienced the pressure of juggling academics, athletics and social life, and have had some rough moments in the process. There are also students who have gone through a special experience or lived with unusual challenges that have had a significant effect on their high school experience.

John, who had always been the butt of fat-boy jokes in middle school, found new social status when he lost pounds and gained friends. In high school he was suddenly so besieged with social dates that his schoolwork took a back seat. His grades plummeted as his social life soared. Realizing at the end of junior year that he was headed for the point of no return, John took a new tack and began to get things together. He managed, by dint of really concerted effort, to bring his grades up to a more respectable level. His early academic record, however, was a disaster. His independent college advisor suggested that in the interview he meet the problem head on by dealing openly with the reasons for his past record and demonstrating that his present grades were a better indication of his ability.

Nora didn't consider her visual impairment a handicap to learning. She kept up with her classmates, played the flute, participated in student government, and had good friends. In the interview she discussed her disability as a personal characteristic, but didn't dwell on it. She focused instead on the abilities that were evident in her record, activities and goals.

All through high school Sarah had actively expressed her liberal point of view. In her junior year she ran into a conservative history teacher who didn't respect opinions that differed markedly from his own. He seemed to take an instant dislike to Sarah's outspokenness, rarely called on her, and sometimes ridiculed her in front of her classmates. He was critical of all her papers and consistently gave her low grades. It was an intolerable situation that began to affect Sarah's work not only in history, but in her other classes as well. The term ended with a marked deterioration in Sarah's grades. In her senior year, Sarah passed with flying colors, but she still had this one bad semester on her transcript, and she thought the history teacher might even have written a negative report for the record. Assuming that she shouldn't complain about a teacher to the admission people, Sarah didn't know how to deal with the problem. After discussing the dilemma with her parents and her school counselor, Sarah decided to lay her cards on the interview table. Her approach was not to whine or gripe, but to explain forthrightly how her liberal viewpoint had clashed with her teacher's conservative ideas, and the overall effect this experience had on her schoolwork. After giving the subject much thought, Sarah was ready to discuss what she had learned about coping with a stressful situation.

All during middle school the tension between Scott's parents had increased until they finally sought a divorce, with Scott a pawn in their battle. Scott was emotionally torn apart. Everything around him seemed to be disintegrating. He struggled to maintain his equilibrium, but he had a hard time keeping his mind on his schoolwork. Eventually, with the help of his close friends and their parents, he got his act together and began salvaging his academic and social life. Having learned a lot about himself, Scott chose to talk about these special circumstances in his interview, providing the admission counselor with a fuller understanding of his background.

Kim's father was in the Navy and was periodically transferred to different posts. Every time they moved, Kim had to cope with a new neighborhood, new friends and a new school. Although none of this came easily, Kim found excitement and adventure in each relocation. She thought that her college interviewer would be interested in her experiences.

Diego had to work every day after school and on weekends and didn't have time to participate in athletics or clubs. His activity sheet was blank except for his jobs. He decided that he would talk about this in his interviews, not as a weakness but as a strength.

Admission counselors are interested in hearing about any special situations that affected you. They want to know how you've handled difficult experiences and about any extra effort you've had to make because of extenuating circumstances.

Not all difficult situations or problem areas are subjects for a college interview, however. Ask a teacher, your parents or an adult close to you to advise whether discussing your particular situation is appropriate.

Practice Interviews

To give you an extra dose of confidence before you venture out for the real thing, try to have a practice interview. Invite a friend to role-play with you, taking turns as the interviewer and the interviewee. Ask a neighbor or a friend of the family to conduct a mock interview. Or perhaps you know someone who does job interviewing who will rehearse with you. You might enjoy videotaping the session. Seeing yourself on video can give you an insight into how you project yourself.

Use the questions in this chapter and in Chapter 16, "Questions Interviewers Ask" and Chapter 17, "Questions to Ask Your Interviewer," as starting points for your practice. Don't, however, memorize a speech and don't prepare so carefully that you sound like a robot. You want to preserve your spontaneity and your ability to respond to the individuality of the interviewer. Remember, you're preparing a concept, not a script. The interviewer wants to meet a prepared student, but not one who has a prepared speech.

One practice strategy that gives you a taste of the real thing is to start your interviews at a college where your admission chances are pretty good. Save the interviews at your "reach" colleges for later when you have gained some experience. (See "Best Timing" in Chapter 14.)

Putting your best foot forward means projecting yourself in a pleasant, polite, thought-through manner that will make you a long-remembered candidate. The better you understand yourself, the more likely you'll be yourself in the interview. When a question comes around requiring you to talk about yourself, you'll be ready. (See Chapter 16, "Questions Interviewers Ask.")

Checklist for Putting Your Best Foot Forward

Know Thyself

❑ Know your academic self

❑ Know the nonacademic you

❑ Know your goals and values

❑ Answer the "Twenty Questions"

❑ Know your Agenda

Shine Through

❑ Be yourself

❑ Be positive

❑ Be honest

❑ Be polite

Don'ts

❑ Don't pose

❑ Don't whisper

❑ Don't be arrogant

❑ Don't memorize

Chapter 14

Planning for the Interview

What to Wear

A few days before the first interview, Andy's father considered buying him a new sports jacket and dress pants so he wouldn't appear at the college in torn jeans and dirty sneakers, but Andy refused to go wearing preppy attire. Margot, however, thought she ought to get dressed up for her visit to the campus, but she wasn't quite sure what that meant. Grace wanted to stand out from the crowd and contemplated wearing her punk outfit and short sleeves to show off her tattoos.

Although dress isn't crucial, it does count. The interviewer's first impression is based on how you look. If Shakespeare was right in stating "apparel oft proclaims the man," then Andy's torn jeans bespoke a careless attitude that was misleading. As much as Andy resented getting cleaned up, and as much as he professed a "take-me-as-I-am" attitude, he had to confess that he wasn't indifferent to the interview.

The importance of clothes is in helping you make a good first impression. Just as you wouldn't wear torn jeans or flashy clothes to a job interview, you shouldn't wear them to a college interview. Feel comfortable and at ease in what you wear, but you aren't going to a picnic or a ball game; so leave your favorite T-shirt at home. Neat and clean are the rules for this trip. Dress for an important meeting, not a dance or a party, and wear clothes suitable for a moderately formal occasion. At the same time, don't wear an outfit right off the rack, as you're probably more comfortable with something tried and true. If you haven't donned a tie and jacket before, this isn't the time to do so.

Your aim is to look and feel your best. If, like Grace, you must make a statement with your clothes, you better be prepared to gab about your garb, as it won't go unnoticed. Your costume might provide just the opening for an interesting conversation about your views on conformity. According to one admission counselor, attitude is quite important: "We won't hold a Mohawk or a Goth style against a student, but we sure would like to know if it's mere self-indulgence." On the other hand, you don't have to "dress for success" in a nondescript uniform. As another counselor put it, "You definitely don't have to wear a shirtwaist dress or a silk tie, but please don't come dressed for a beach party, wearing sunglasses and chewing gum."

In general, pressed khakis, a clean, quiet dress shirt (with or without a tie) or an unwrinkled polo and a sweater or a jacket are appropriate for men. Shoes are better than sneakers, and all laces should be tied. One admission counselor from a mid-Atlantic college warns: "Sloppy doesn't cut the mustard here. Nobody minds jeans and a sweater as long as they're neat and clean, but for heaven's sake, tie your shoelaces, wear some socks and don't come in flip-flops."

A skirt or pants, a neat blouse with a jacket or sweater or a simple dress in a subdued color are suitable for women. Jewelry, such as earrings, should be tasteful, and shoes should fit the apparel and be neither too dressy nor too informal. Try to have a put-together look. A Midwestern admission counselor advises: "Clothes do make a difference. Artsy clothes are fine, but ripped-up jeans a no-no. We don't require a uniform, but we do like to think you've put some thought into your appearance."

Mind Your P's and Q's

Having planned your outfit, there are now some other matters to attend to in preparation for the interview. These include:

The Three P's	The Two Q's
1. Be prepared	1. Don't quibble or complain
2. Be prompt	2. Ask questions
3. Be polite	

Be Prepared

One of the points that admission counselors across the country agree on is that students should come prepared. Admission people enjoy talking to students who have given the college and the interview some real thought. This means knowing beforehand as much about the college as possible. You'll be well-informed if you study the college's website (see Chapter 8, "Surfing and Decoding a College Website") and jot down any questions you have. Doug wanted to clarify the academic requirements for a foreign language and Jeff the opportunities for study abroad. Emma asked about the strengths of the film department and Mandy the number of women graduates who were accepted into law school.

As you tour the campus, other issues will come up. You may be interested in how to get on the newspaper staff without majoring in journalism, how the college chooses freshman roommates, what services there are for the visually impaired, the role fraternities play or the economic diversity of the students. All these subjects indicate your interest in delving deeper into the character of the college.

Admission counselors always enjoy meeting students who ask discerning questions not already answered on the website. (See Chapter 17, "Questions to Ask Your Interviewer.")

Another way to prepare is to know yourself. (See Chapter 13, "Putting Your Best Foot Forward.") Understand your strengths, special qualities, talents, values and goals, and be aware of your weaknesses. Be ready to talk about yourself and not like a steamroller or in a whisper, but clearly and distinctly in your natural voice. If you clam up or answer in monosyllables, the interviewer won't learn much about you. Practice talking in sentences and paragraphs, and learn to describe what is important to you. This is not the time to keep your good points under wraps.

Admission interviewers appreciate talking to students who aren't echoes of other students. Do your homework to understand both yourself and the college, project your special qualities and you'll be a hit.

Be Prompt

It goes without saying, be on time for your interview. Plan to reach the admission office five to 10 minutes before the scheduled appointment. Use this interval to freshen up, think about the points you want to make, collect your thoughts and then walk into the interview relaxed and confident. Your interview may last as long as an hour, so don't set up another appointment or arrange your ride to the airport without giving yourself plenty of time. Allow time to mull over the interview in a quiet place before you proceed to your next destination.

Be Polite

Bring your best manners with you to the interview. If the interviewer offers his or her hand, shake it firmly. Your handshake and your clothes are the first quick impressions the counselor has, so don't be limp as a dishrag or use a vise grip. Practice at home if necessary.

Wait until you're asked to sit down and then sit up straight (not ramrod straight, just easy straight). Be relaxed, but don't slump, sprawl or lean into the interviewer so that you are nose to nose. Show you're ready to talk by your alert, respectful attitude. Address the interviewer by name, or "sir" or "ma'am" if that is comfortable for you. Don't smoke. Don't chew gum. Don't swear. Do turn off your cell phone.

Interviewers are skilled at putting you at ease, but each has a different style and personality. If the interviewer's approach is to tell jokes, smile or laugh if you wish, but don't think you have to. Above all, don't try to compete in the joke category. You may not hit it off with all the interviewers you meet, so don't panic if things aren't going as well as you'd hoped. Sometimes it's the interviewer who's having a bad day, not you.

The interviewer will signal that the end of the session is near by making a wrap-up statement, pulling papers together, getting up and motioning for you to do the same or saying something to that effect. Don't begin talking suddenly about a new subject or try to continue the conversation. If you have more questions, ask the counselor if you might pose them in an email. Create the right impression with a pleasant, straightforward manner, a firm handshake and a polite thank-you.

When you get home, write a note or send an email asking those unanswered questions, clarifying a point or commenting on your visit. One admission counselor considers notes a confirmation of good manners; another appreciates them so much he files them in a "We Love You" folder. Counselors genuinely like to hear from you, and it informs them of your interest in the college.

Don't Quibble or Complain

Don't pick a fight with the interviewer. Don't walk into the interview with a chip on your shoulder. This isn't the moment to correct the counselor's grammar or quibble about the pronunciation of a word. If there is a controversy, stand up for your point of view, but be tactful and courteous.

Don't complain about all the wrongs done to you. Don't be like Albert, who blamed his math teachers for his bad marks, or Stella, who thought her chemistry teacher had it in for her. Both were ready to accuse their teachers and excuse themselves — don't you do the same. If there is a special circumstance that needs explaining, present it in a straightforward manner so that both you and the teacher share the involvement. A good motto to bring with you is: Accentuate the positive; eliminate the negative.

Take responsibility for the grades you received unless there are extraordinary, extenuating circumstances. Occasionally, you may get into a situation where you and a teacher have just not seen eye to eye. Analyze the situation beforehand and see if you can come up with a forthright way to deal with it, as Sarah did. (See Chapter 13, "Putting Your Best Foot Forward.")

Ask Questions

One of your principal objectives in the interview is to find out more about the college. Don't be afraid to ask anything and everything you want to know — making sure, of course, that the answers you seek aren't available in the literature the college has sent you or on the college website. There's no sense in asking if there's an anthropology department when you can look it up.

Don't ask questions just for the sake of asking or pose as an expert in something you know little about. Interviewers are plenty savvy. Having spoken with hundreds of students, they can spot show-off and off-the-wall questions asked merely for effect.

Admission counselors agree that probing questions that challenge them to think often point out a candidate's specialness. As a college shopper you must be curious. Explore your concerns, and then, without hesitation, ask questions that are relevant. You undoubtedly have found ideas in Part I, and you may get other thoughts when you read Chapter 17, "Questions to Ask Your Interviewer."

It's okay to have a list of questions with you and refer to them as the conversation proceeds. Otherwise, know in advance what your queries are and review them in your head before the interview. Be inquiring. You are making an expensive, important investment that you want to be sure will benefit you. You wouldn't invest in a tablet or computer without asking the dealer lots of questions. Handle the college interview just as inquisitively.

Best Timing

When making plans for your interviews, remember: "likelies first." Gain experience at your "likely" schools where the interview won't make a crucial difference and you can be more relaxed.

Schedule interviews at your most desired colleges for somewhere near the end of the line when you'll be "interview seasoned," and remember to book your appointments well ahead of time because interview schedules fill up early. It is best to make your appointments in the summer for the following fall, especially at popular colleges.

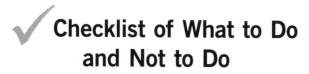

Checklist of What to Do and Not to Do

Do	Don't
❏ Be neat, clean and comfortable	❏ Smoke, swear or chew gum
❏ Look and feel your best	❏ Quibble or complain
❏ Be prepared, prompt and polite	❏ Pose
❏ Ask informed questions	❏ Be passive
❏ Accentuate the positive	❏ Whisper
❏ Be yourself	❏ Be arrogant
❏ Turn off your cell phone	
❏ Send a thank-you note or email on your return home	

Try to arrange your interview toward the end of your campus visit to give yourself ample chance to look around and talk to students. Your impressions and questions will be fresh and you will have a number of things to discuss with the interviewer. (See "An Ideal Campus Schedule" in Chapter 4.)

Special Hints

- Don't become weary, complacent or bored because of a heavy interview schedule. If you think you're losing your zest, take a break and regroup. Few things are as much of a turnoff to interviewers as a bored student or a know-it-all. When you arrive at your first-choice college, you should be confident and in good spirits.

- Don't bring your super term paper, poetry selections or other long pieces of writing with you. You want the interview to be a conversation, not a reading session. Send all your special extras as a supplement to your application.

- Don't hand over your transcript or résumé to the interviewer unless it is asked for or you have a special reason to discuss it.

After the Interview Is Over

It's always a good idea to sit down in a quiet place and review how the interview went. If you missed some good openings or didn't get across some important points, you can follow up with an email. Think about ways you can avoid letting that happen in future interviews. Don't worry if you think the interview didn't go just right; not all interviews will be four-star experiences, and you are probably your own worst critic. Remember, also, that the interview isn't the only, or the most important, aspect of your application. Do your part by preparing for the interview and feeling comfortable being yourself and things will go well.

When you get home, remember to send an email thanking the interviewer and any other important people you met with. (For sample emails, see Chapter 4, "Making Arrangements.")

Chapter 15

Tips for
the Shy Person

The Problem

Ever since he could remember, George tried to disappear into his surroundings and avoid being "put on the spot." He never raised his hand in class; he blushed when he was called upon to speak; he couldn't tell a joke or laugh at himself and his stomach went into knots at parties. He was especially unsure of himself in new situations.

With college time approaching, and with it the necessity of talking to complete strangers on campus visits and in interviews, George almost panicked. His normal fear of new situations was intensified by the frightening prospect of revealing himself to people he didn't know. George assumed he would be a failure, stammering and blushing during the interview and walking around each new campus without talking to a soul. All his life he had tried to hide his shyness, but he knew that for his college search he would be compelled to deal with it or face the prospect of not applying to colleges where visits and interviews were important. That would limit his chances of making the right college choice.

George's concerns are typical of a shy person, but he is not alone. Almost everyone has experienced some degree of shyness in new situations. Some people hang back in social encounters, feeling ill at ease in a room full of strangers, waiting for someone else to take the lead.

Others may experience a mild physical reaction such as damp palms, a dry mouth or a rapid heartbeat. In *The Shy Person's Book*, Claire Rayner says that those with a greater degree of shyness display reactions that range from a parched throat to a voice so low that it cannot be heard; from squeaking to stammering; from mild to severe perspiring; from going pale to blushing; from a thick lumping in the throat to a relentless thumping in the chest to a bobbing head caused by severe neck tremors. Some talk so much at a high speed that they cannot be interrupted; others adopt a blustery, hale and hearty manner to try to hide inner nervousness.

George's reactions were on the extreme end of the scale. In everyday new situations he had so much trouble keeping his physical symptoms under control that he sometimes didn't even hear what people said to him. In the interview, he feared he wouldn't know what to say if he was asked a direct question, or worse, he would make a fool of himself by saying something silly. He dreaded not only the interviews, but the campus visit as well. The mere notion of wandering about a strange place and staying overnight with someone he didn't know made him panicky. Although George didn't want to surrender his option of having good college choices, he didn't know how to cope with his problem. He tried to forget it, but it wouldn't go away. George finally decided to talk to his parents about his painful predicament. After quietly listening to his disturbing account, his parents helped George organize a plan.

Acknowledging the Problem

Discussing his problem with his parents was a good decision. The first step toward overcoming shyness is to acknowledge it. The second step is to want to change. Once faced, there are ways to deal with it. Shy people differ not so much in the degree of shyness they suffer from, but in how each copes with his or her problem.

If you think you share elements of George's uneasiness in facing the campus visit and the interview, here are some ways to prepare yourself.

Practice Talking

If you are fortunate enough to have someone, a friend or a relative, with whom you can share this difficulty, set up some situations where you talk about yourself on a steady basis. It is important that you practice talking aloud about yourself, for that's what you'll be doing in the interview. Speak about a project you're working on, a paper you're writing or a problem in school. Begin with information about the topic and move into how you feel about it, how it is relevant to you. Put yourself into the information. What do you like about the project? What did you learn from the subject? State something about the topic that interests you. Practice speaking in the first-person singular. Use the words, "I think," "I feel" or "This is the way it strikes me." Don't be afraid that you'll be boring. And remember that it will take time to feel comfortable communicating with another person, especially if you've been avoiding such situations.

To help George become accustomed to talking about himself, his parents launched "take a topic to dinner." Every night they encouraged George to talk about a school event. At first he was halting and uncomfortable, but gradually he began to unwind. When he became more at ease, they suggested more complex topics such as hopes for the future or goals that each member of the family wanted to achieve. George's two older brothers, who usually monopolized the mealtime conversation, began listening to George and talking with him instead of at him. Pretty soon the family began having shared dinner conversations with George as a participant rather than a full-time silent listener. Still later, his parents suggested that each person tell a joke, and they helped George overcome his awkwardness by having him read the joke aloud first. Getting this kind of practice helped George acquire self-confidence, which loosened his tensions about talking about himself.

Strategies for Those with No One to Turn To

George was lucky that he had family support in his efforts to handle his shyness, but not everyone is that fortunate. If you don't have someone with whom you can talk, there are other approaches you can take, but remember, they take time, patience and practice.

One measure is to write down your statement about a project, paper or school problem and then read it aloud in front of a mirror or an empty chair. Put the paper away and speak your piece. Try this several times a week. Write about a different topic and follow the same procedure the next week. Don't forget to put yourself into the statement. Use the first-person singular. Even though you may feel silly doing this, it will give you practice talking out loud about yourself.

If you have a video recorder, you might want to record your statement. Talking into a recorder simulates, in a small way, the experience of talking to an audience. It also helps to hear how you sound, but don't be shocked by hearing your voice for the first time. Most people don't like hearing their own voice at first.

After you have read your written statements about a school issue several times, practice talking about a personal experience. Speak aloud about something that happened to you at school. Talk to the mirror or chair. If something funny happened, don't be afraid to verbalize it. Do this activity several times.

Next, state a belief that is important to you. Speak in the first person. Express out loud the feelings and experiences that led you to this belief. Personal beliefs might include the importance of your family, or what you think about honesty, or the value of friendship or religion. Whatever your beliefs, articulating them will help you better present what you've learned about who you are and what makes you tick. Continue these activities every day. Don't give up.

Another technique is to keep a journal detailing the events of the day. Read the entry aloud in front of a mirror. Get accustomed to hearing your voice say "I." Practice, practice, practice talking aloud.

These exercises will boost your ability to talk about yourself and give you the confidence to present yourself at your strongest in the interview.

Other Tips

To enable you to become more comfortable speaking to strangers, the outstanding expert Philip Zimbardo, in his book *Shyness*, recommends practicing talking on the phone. He suggests calling a local store and checking on the price of an advertised item, calling a movie theater and asking for show times or calling the library and asking the reference librarian what the population of the United States is or any other information you'd like to know.

Books on shyness also recommend talking to strangers in safe, public places. One tactic is to speak to a salesperson in a store. Ask about how an item works or what other colors it comes in, and spend at least 30 seconds talking. Another approach is to go to the library and ask a librarian where the college directories are and tell her why you are looking. Don't be afraid to say, "I'm a senior in high school beginning my college search, and I need some help."

Still another recommended exercise in safely talking to a stranger can take place when you're in the check-out line of a store, by striking up a conversation about a common experience you are sharing. Talk to the clerk or the person behind you about the weather, or the crowds or the lack of crowds. An opening remark might be a positive statement such as, "It's such a nice day! It makes me want to be out hiking in the country." Or, "I like shopping in this store. The salespeople are so pleasant." Other places where you can practice overcoming shyness are movie lines, the school cafeteria or sports events.

The Bowers, authors of *Asserting Yourself*, suggest writing down facts about each of these "greeting-talk" conversations: (1) where it took place, (2) with whom, (3) what you said, (4) what the other person said, (5) what your reactions were, (6) how you felt about yourself. This will help you clue into what really happens in public socializing.

Another way to learn to express yourself vocally is to go up after class and ask a teacher about an assignment, or about a theme you wrote or about anything else that is relevant. Practice out loud what you'll say beforehand, but don't memorize a script. If you feel more confident writing it down in advance, just scribble a few key words, not whole sentences.

If there is a particular teacher who you think may be sympathetic, try enlisting his or her help. Explain your problem and what you're doing to overcome it. Perhaps the teacher will have helpful suggestions.

Other places where talking is a necessity are drama clubs, speech classes and forensics societies. If your school or community has one of these groups, investigate and see if you want to join. You may first have to overcome some of your apprehensions, but it might prove to be just the ticket.

People who deal with shyness recommend learning a joke, writing it down, and then practicing it out loud to yourself. After you have mastered it, tell it to a friend or a small group of people.

Remember that the objective of these exercises is getting accustomed to talking out loud and communicating with others. It won't happen overnight, and you have to practice.

Books and Websites

Listed below are several books that suggest useful ways to deal with shyness; your library may have others.

Bower, Sharon Anthony and Gordon H. 2004. *Asserting Yourself.* Cambridge, Mass.: Da Capo Press.

Desberg, Peter. 1996. *No More Butterflies.* Oakland, Calif.: New Harbinger Publications, Inc.

Phillips, Gerald M. 1988. *Help for Shy People.* New York, N.Y.: Sterling Publishing.

Rayner, Claire. 1974. *The Shy Person's Book.* New York, N.Y.: D. McKay Co.

Wassmer, Arthur C. 1978. *Making Contact.* New York, N.Y.: Dial Press.

Zimbardo, Philip G. 1990. *Shyness: What It Is, What to Do About It.* Cambridge, Mass.: Da Capo Press.

In addition, there are several websites devoted to shyness that may be helpful. One site run by The Shyness Institute is www.shyness.com, and a master website listing resources for shyness is at www.shakeyourshyness.com.

Dealing with Questions

Once you feel somewhat more at ease talking about yourself to other people, you can begin to tackle the give-and-take of the interview process. Explore the questions in Chapters 13 and 16, paying particular attention to those that are more personal in nature. Get a handle on the areas you find difficult to talk about; then concentrate on thinking these through. Write down your answers to these questions so that they make sense. Say them aloud in front of a mirror and practice looking yourself in the eye.

To get the feel of an interview from both sides of the desk, have a friend or relative do a mock interview with you and take turns playing the parts of interviewer and interviewee. The experts on shyness find that role-playing helps one acclimate to new situations. Use the questions you have worked on and continue with new ones. Don't memorize your answers, but work up to extemporizing. If this part comes too hard, go back to square one and talk about an activity important to you.

Other Steps to Take

Shy people sometimes put others off physically by not appearing receptive. You can learn how to change this. One authority on shyness, Dr. Arthur C. Wassmer, recommends practicing making eye contact by concentrating on looking directly at the person with whom you're talking. Looking at a person is an indication that you are *interested* and that you are paying attention.

Another of Dr. Wassmer's recommendations is to practice smiling and nodding your head in response, indicating your interest. He also suggests sitting in a relaxed posture with hands in your lap or on the chair arms, not folded across your chest. As you do these exercises, look at the person, smile at appropriate times, nod your head in approval of a particular statement and sit in a relaxed posture.

Relaxation Techniques

Shy people are not the only ones nervous about the interview. Almost every student experiences some anxiety before the interview actually begins. The first 15 seconds of an interview are usually the hardest, and the interviewer is aware that the first task is to put you at ease. Remember that the interviewer wants to talk to you and wants to help you talk about yourself.

People who deal with stress suggest that each of us learns how to relax in tense situations. One of the common ways to deal with tension is to do deep breathing as follows: Take three deep breaths, using your abdominal muscles. Count to five as you breathe in, hold briefly, then breathe out in five counts. At the end of each sequence say to yourself, "om," or "easy does it." Try this now to see if you feel more relaxed. Practice to see if you're comfortable breathing this way.

If the deep breathing isn't comfortable for you, try sitting in a relaxed position and then concentrate on breathing naturally. Breathe in and out, in and out, saying "om" to yourself after each sequence. If your mind starts wandering, bring it back to your breathing. This exercise often has the effect of easing tension.

Keep in Mind

Remember that the college interviewer is interested in you. He or she wants to make contact with you and is skilled in drawing you out. You must develop a willingness and desire to respond. By exploring your interests and activities — anything from graphic novels to baseball to music — and learning to talk about them, you will have more confidence when the interview takes place. Systematically read the preceding chapters on the interview, taking notes, following directions and setting goals.

If you experience severe shyness during the interview and things aren't going well, a good solution is to acknowledge it and tell the interviewer how you feel. You will probably find the interviewer receptive to you saying something like, "I'm really uncomfortable now. I'm trying to overcome my shyness, but it's hard for me to talk right at this moment." You'll be pleasantly relieved at the way most interviewers will react. However, if the interviewer is a cold fish, nothing much is going to help. You'll have to chalk that one up to experience.

When Nothing Else Works

If you find that none of these measures works for you, you may want to consult with your physician. Your doctor may prescribe a medication that actors sometimes use to block the symptoms of stage fright.

A Special Hint

More than others, the shy person needs to plan everything well in advance and follow through on the arrangements. Carefully study Chapters 3, 4 and 5 for the general outline of preparations to make and things to do. If you cannot do them yourself, and many shy people cannot, enlist your parents to assist in the preparations, making the necessary phone calls, for example. Don't be ashamed to ask your family for help. Remember that the goal is to enable the college to know the real you despite your shyness.

Checklist for the Shy Person

❏ Review your strengths and interests. Know why you are interested in this college.

❏ Call in advance for the interview appointment. Make sure you write down the day and time.

❏ Ask where the meeting is going to take place and with whom. Become familiar with your interviewer's name.

❏ If the interview is to take place on campus and you haven't visited before, look on the college website, print out the campus map and highlight the admission office.

❏ Get directions.

❏ Arrange to go with your parents, grandparents, a favorite relative or a friend — whoever is supportive and makes you most comfortable.

❏ Bring a list of written questions. Refer to the list whenever necessary.

❏ Dress appropriately.

❏ Arrive on time.

❏ Make eye contact.

❏ Shake hands firmly.

❏ Do not interrupt.

❏ Stay attentive.

❏ Most importantly, practice the above before the interview.

Chapter 16

Questions Interviewers Ask

"What will they ask? What kinds of questions will they stick to me? How will I know what to say?" These are the worrisome fears that most students have about the interview. By the time you reach this chapter, you should have a good notion of what the interview is all about and realize that the questions are not intended to "catch you" but rather to help you talk about yourself. Remember that one purpose of the interview is to get to know you better, and questions are a way to break the ice and get you started.

In the first few minutes of warm-up time the admission counselor, knowing that it is a strained situation, tries to put you at ease. He or she might begin with a few social amenities and pleasantries that may give you information about his or her role in the college or the intent and direction of the interview. If the counselor already has some information about you, he or she may comment on it.

Question Categories

A standard interview then goes on to its main purpose: for the interviewer to learn more about you and for you to learn more about the college. The questions are up to the individual interviewer, but each one tries to deal with three areas:

1.   Your high school years: your academic, extracurricular and community experiences
2.   College in general, and the college you are visiting specifically
3.   You and the world around you

The following sections provide sample questions on these subjects that have been asked at a variety of colleges to get interviews under way. An interviewer will sometimes ask only one or two of these questions as a springboard to get things rolling. These questions should not be answered with a curt yes or no. The questions are meant to draw you out so that the conversation, led by a skilled admission counselor, will flow from area to area.

Mull over these questions. Practice elaborating on your thinking. Think about the whys of your reactions. Formulate your responses by using your Agenda and reviewing the "Twenty Questions," both found in Chapter 13. Practice talking out loud to your family or friends. *Don't memorize.* Your purpose in reflecting about these questions is to clarify your thoughts on these subjects, not to write a script.

Questions About Your High School Experience

The questions about high school touch topics you are most familiar with: your academic background, your thoughts about high school, extracurricular activities and your community.

Your Academic Background and School

- Tell me about your high school.

- Tell me something about your courses. Do you have a favorite? An un-favorite?

- What subjects have you enjoyed the most?

- What courses have been most difficult for you?

- What is your high school schedule? Why did you choose these classes?

- What satisfactions have you had from your studies?

- Has school been challenging? What course has been most challenging?

- Have you gone beyond the required assignment in any subject?

- What kind of student have you been? Would this change if you had the chance to do it over again?

- Have you worked up to your potential?

- Is your record an accurate gauge of your abilities and potential?

- Is there any outside circumstance that interfered with your academic performance?

- Do you like your high school?

- How would you describe your school?

- What is the range of students at your school? Where do you fit in?

- Do you like your teachers? Do you have a favorite teacher? Tell me about him/her.

- What has been a controversial issue in your school? What is your reaction to the controversy?

- If you had the chance, what changes would you make in your school?

Your Extracurricular Activities

- What extracurricular activity has been the most satisfying to you? The most fun?

- What is the most significant contribution you've made to your school?

- How would others describe your role in the school community?

- What activities do you enjoy most outside the daily routine of school?

- Do you have any hobbies or special interests?

- Have you worked or been a volunteer?

- Would you make different choices if you were to do it all over again?

- What do you most enjoy doing for fun? For relaxation? For stimulation?

- How do you spend a typical day after school?

- How much time do you spend on Facebook?

- What do you do in your spare time?

- How did you spend last summer? What are your plans for this coming summer?

- What do you do with any money you've earned?

- Is there any activity that you want to explore at college?

Your Community

- How would you describe your hometown?

- Tell me something about your community.

- What has been a controversial issue in your community? Do you have a position on it?

- How has living in your community affected your outlook?

Questions About College

The second category of questions is about college. The two basic questions, ones that you should give some real thought to, are *Why do you want to go to college?* and *Why are you interested in this college?* There are variations on this theme that require further analysis, so try to think beyond the "getting a good education" response or "finding a career." Think a little harder and dig a little deeper to get answers that are true for you. For "why this college?" you need to have researched the school and know why it appeals to you.

Corollaries to these questions are:

- What satisfactions do you expect to find in college?

- What are you looking forward to in college?

- What do you hope to accomplish in the next four years?

- What do you expect to get out of college?

- What do you want from an education?

- What knowledge are you seeking?

- What interests do you want to pursue in college?

- What do you hope to major in and why?

- What self-development do you see for yourself in college?

- What are some of your criteria or considerations in choosing a college?

The following are questions that deal directly with the college you are visiting. Be sure you are prepared to talk and ask questions about this college.

- Why do you think you're a good fit for our college?

- Why do you want to come here?

- How did you first hear about us?

- What do you want to know about us?

- What is of most interest to you on campus?

- Has anything surprised you?

- What other colleges are you considering?

- What is your dream job?

- What do you expect to be doing seven years from now? Twelve years? Twenty years?

- Have you ever thought of not going to college? What would you do?

Questions About You and the World Around You

This third category of questions requires some soul-searching. The interviewer doesn't ask such questions to provoke you, but to dig a little deeper into your attitudes and viewpoint. This category includes what are generally appreciated as the "hard" questions, which often include some type of book question, a variation on the hero or heroine theme, more probing personal queries and current event topics. The more selective the college, the more searching these questions tend to be. The following are sample questions, but recognize that there are as many questions as there are interviewers. However, if you can handle the following list, you'll be prepared for almost anything. Be sure you're responding with your own ideas and enthusiasms. Don't get into a hole by talking about a book you merely skimmed or a topic you're not informed about. Try out the questions, giving them some well-honed thought.

Book Questions

Always *be prepared* for a book question.

- What are you reading now that isn't an assigned book?

- What are you reading that is of interest to you?

- Are there any books you've read in the last year or so that significantly affected you?

- What is the best book you've ever read?

- What three books would you take to a desert island?

- Are there any authors you particularly like?

- Any literary character you admire?

- What magazines do you read regularly?

- What TV shows do you watch?

- What are your favorite movies?

- What play, concert, museum exhibit or dance recital have you recently attended? What is your opinion of it?

Hero or Heroine Questions

- Do you have any contemporary heroes?

- Do you have any historical heroes?

- What person, living or dead, would you most like to talk to and what would you talk about?

- What person has had the greatest impact in this century?

- What president would you most like to meet? Why?

- Is there any person who has had a great influence on you?

Personal Questions

- What things do you do well? What are your talents?

- Tell me something about your family.

- Tell me about your upbringing. What things are important to your parents? On what issues do you have differences?

- What are some good decisions you've made for yourself recently?

- How would you describe your friendships?

- How would your best friend describe you? Would you agree?

- What three adjectives would you use to describe yourself?

- What three wishes do you have?

- What are your strengths? Your weaknesses?

- What pressures do you feel to conform? How have you gone your own way?

- What do you think sets you apart as an individual in your school?

- Tell me about a person, an event or an experience that has had an impact on you.

- What difficult situation have you been in, and how did you resolve it?

- What is the most difficult situation you've had to face?

- How would you describe your most intellectually stimulating experience?

- Of what accomplishments are you most proud?

Current Events

- What political or social issues should a young person be interested in?

- What do you think about drug and alcohol use, gun control, the death penalty, nuclear power, marijuana laws, school vouchers, standardized tests, terrorism, the latest headline?

- Do you ever become indignant about anything happening in the world?

- If you were President of the United States, what would you do about a current controversial issue?

- What historical event has had the most impact on this century?

- If you had the political power to do anything you wanted, what would you do?

Dealing with the Unexpected and Provocative

From time to time you may run across an interviewer whose style is to be provocative and to ask curveball questions. There isn't any way to prepare for the surprise question except to recognize that the possibility exists and that it is more likely to occur at the most selective colleges. Such interviews may be more stressful because they aggressively challenge you and test how you respond. Lynne A. Sarikes of Northeastern University says "[This is a way of] catching you a little off guard to see how you think." The following may sound like unlikely questions, but, in fact, they have been asked.

- What do you think you can do for this college?

- It is 25 years from now. What will you do tomorrow?

- What would you do if you had a "do over" button?

- In a news story about your life, what would the headline be?

- Tell me about an article you've read in the past few days from a magazine, newspaper or online.

- There's an invisible box on my desk with things in it that describe you. What's in the box?

- What would you like to talk about?

- If you could be a fruit, an animal, a character in fiction, what or who would you be?

- If you could be a superhero, what powers would you want?

But even these questions shouldn't be threatening if you've done your homework preparing for the interview. Review the previous chapters and you'll have methods for dealing with this type of question. And bear in mind when under stress:

- Keep your responses honest. Don't try to fake anything.

- Keep cool. Take a deep breath and remain composed. Stressful questions reveal the interviewer's personality more than yours.

- If you don't understand the question, ask what the interviewer means.

- Don't pose as an expert on matters you know little about. It's okay to say, "I don't know."

- You can say, "I've never thought about that. I'll have to mull it over. Is it okay if I email you about this?"

- Be courteous and tactful.

If you think you really haven't been given a fair shake by an intense and grilling interviewer, you may email the dean of admission and request another interview with a different member of the admission staff. Make sure you have correctly evaluated the situation and can back up your statement with examples.

Chapter 17

Questions to Ask Your Interviewer

Why Ask Questions?

Jeff was surprised that after he had answered several questions, his interviewer asked if he had any questions. Jeff drew a blank and said that he was satisfied that all his questions had been answered by the tour guide and Professor Emerson, with whom he had met. After leaving the office, Jeff realized that he had missed his chance to talk about his work as coach of a Special Olympics team.

When confronted with the same question, Margot mumbled something about wondering if the weather was always frigid in the winter. She knew this question was empty-headed, but she wasn't prepared for this question about questions.

On the other hand, Luke, who had a sincere interest in doing community service, asked whether there was a soup kitchen near campus where students could volunteer. Anand asked if Indian food was ever served in the dining hall or whether there were any Indian restaurants in the area. Cassie asked if it would be difficult for her to organize an all-women drama club and how hard it might be to schedule performances.

Jeff and Margot were right: they had missed an opportunity to tell the interviewer more about themselves, while Luke and Cassie showed that they were ready to hit the ground running when they got to college. The interviewer also learned something about them that hadn't come through in the other parts of the interview. Anand had a legitimate question about whether someone of his background would feel comfortable at this particular college, and he asked it in a way that wouldn't make the interviewer think he was unhappy with what he had seen.

All students should have questions about the colleges they visit, and those having interviews should be ready for the chance to ask specific questions. Most interviewers will ask if there is anything else you want to know, and this is your chance, and a great opportunity, if you are prepared for it. As a competent college shopper you facilitate your search by asking questions. You wouldn't purchase anything expensive for yourself like a smartphone, computer or car without researching it and querying the salesperson about its quality, characteristics and limitations.

Similarly, you must think about college as something you are buying for yourself that is more expensive and important than any of these other items. It is probably one of the more significant purchases of your shopping life. Before you pay the college bursar's fee, you want to know as much as possible about what you're buying. The college visit is your shopping trip, and the admission counselor is the authority on the who's, whys and how's of the college community. See Chapter 6, "Chief Aspects of College Life," for a way to organize your thoughts and see if there are some questions there that are of particular interest to you.

In fact, college admission counselors genuinely enjoy talking to students. They particularly like students who have thought about the college and who want to know more about it than is in the viewbook or website. They appreciate the challenge of thoughtful questions. This doesn't mean being aggressive or arrogant, nor does it mean asking questions that are smart-alecky or for effect only. It does mean asking questions that add to your understanding of the college, are of genuine interest to you and that haven't been answered by your research, tour or information session. Your questions, and the discussion that well may follow, will help you find out more about the college and will help the interviewer learn something important about you.

Just as you have prepared for the interview (Chapter 13, "Putting Your Best Foot Forward") and know from your Agenda what you want the interviewer to learn about you, you also should be prepared with two or three questions that have relevance to you and your interests, as Cassie and Luke did. Sometimes your questions will be answered during the interview, so be flexible. The questions should be specific to your interests and the best questions will give the interviewer more information than she or he knew before. When you are prepared for asking questions, you are in control. This is a great time to mention something that hasn't been covered in your Agenda. It may further a discussion of something you hadn't had time to go into that was important to you. Try to be ready with the best questions you can, but have a general question or two in your back pocket if you aren't ready to ask something specifically tailored to your Agenda.

After reviewing some of the questions below and adapting one to her own situation, Liz found out that she could tutor students through a program with the local Boys and Girls Club near the college she was interviewing at. Warren, who played lacrosse every Sunday, discovered that there was a lacrosse team. Both Liz and Warren were able to convey part of their Agenda to the interviewer and also discover information that might ultimately help them decide on which college they would attend.

Following are lists with of lots of questions, but it is important that you think about how you can best convey your interests. Some of these questions are generic and the answers may sometimes be found on the college's website. You should be careful about asking such questions if the answers are easily found elsewhere. But these may be just the questions to help your thinking about whether the college is the right one for you. Other questions are appropriate only if their specific content is relevant to you. For instance, asking where you can get a haircut is not particularly appropriate to a person with straight hair, but might be a telling question if there is an ethnic style that the student wears.

Social Life and Campus Activities

Students are the ones who are actively involved with the social life on campus, so most of your questions in this category should be directed to them, as discussed in Chapter 6, "Chief Aspects of College Life." The admission counselor may see social life in a different light, and it may be valuable to get that viewpoint.

After explaining what you like to do for fun, you can ask:

- What do students do for fun?

- What happens on weekends?

- What percentage of students leave campus on the weekends? (If more than 20 percent, ask why.)

If you're interested in joining the same fraternity that your father belonged to, or are worried that fraternities and sororities dominate the social scene, you might ask:

- What is the role of fraternities and sororities on campus?

- Have there been any recent incidents concerning Greek life that I should know about?

- Are the Greek societies open to everyone who wants to pledge?

- Has the administration placed any restrictions on hazing and initiation rites?

- If you didn't want to join, would you have a satisfactory social life?

You might also want to ask about the sports scene and campus events:

- What role do team sports play in the social life of the college?

- What happens on football or basketball weekends?

- If you didn't want to join in, would you find other kindred spirits?

- What were the social or cultural highlights last year?

- Who were some of the speakers who came to campus?

Campus Facilities

The areas to cover in your questions are housing, dining, activity centers and athletic and recreational facilities, health, counseling, career, special student services, miscellaneous, and the library. See Chapter 6, "Chief Aspects of College Life," and all its questions.

Housing

- Is there something I should know about housing here that would help me in my choice?

- How does the college choose freshman roommates?

- Does the college provide housing for all four years?

- What choices will I have as a freshman? As a sophomore? As a senior?

- Which houses are quiet enough for studying? Where else do people study?

- Do certain students tend to live in particular residence halls, i.e., athletes, honors students?

- What special interest houses are there on campus?

Dining *strike resolved*

- What is your opinion about which meal plan is the best value?

- Are there meals for people who are vegetarians? Vegans? Kosher? Halal?

- Are there snack bars and coffeehouses? May students cook in their rooms?

- What is a good place to eat when I leave campus today?

Activity Centers and Athletic and Recreational Facilities

How late is the fitness center open? Are there times when only the varsity teams use the facilities?

- If I didn't major in music or art, would I have access to practice rooms and art studios? What arrangements would I have to make for their use?

- Are any new facilities being planned?

- Is there anything special I should see before I leave?

Security and Technology

- What security measures has the college provided for students at night?

- Is security necessary in the dorms? Have there been any problems?

- Does it matter if I use a Mac instead of a PC?

- What kind of technical support is available?

The Library

- Does the library have special hours during reading and exam week?

- Is there room for everyone who wants to study there?

- Can I reserve books online?

The Community Off Campus

- Is it easy to get public transportation into the city? Where would I catch the bus?

- Is it easy to volunteer at a soup kitchen or to tutor local students? Is there a program already set up for doing this?

- Are there jobs or internships in town for students?

Open Season on Questions

Now you have a good start on the kinds of questions you should be pondering. You may have more interest in a particular category, so concentrate on that area and think about what *you* want to know. It's open season on questions, so ask about anything that concerns you. Don't neglect areas that will affect your college experience. The more you know about a college, the better able you'll be to judge its qualities.

As you walk around campus and speak to students, faculty and admission staff, you'll get the answers to many of your queries. Keep notes. When you return home, sort out your impressions, using your "College Evaluation Checklist" in Chapter 10 as a guide. If you don't get a chance to find out all you want to know in the interview, email your interviewer. Admission counselors welcome good questions and are always interested in helping you become better informed, and they are pleased when they receive your questions or your thank-you note.

Jeff, who had wished he had mentioned his involvement with Special Olympics, wrote a note within a week of his visit and mentioned his coaching work and asked if there was already a club on campus. Margot helped herself by emailing her interviewer to say how much she enjoyed her visit.

Chapter 18

Summing Up

When Emma and Jeff met again in the student center snack bar to talk about their day and overnight at Burgess, Emma was glowing, but Jeff was somewhat more subdued.

Although the interviews had gone well for Jeff, he had encountered some troubling drawbacks. Along with an anti-fraternity bias, he had found much more academic pressure than he thought he wanted. He had also detected a lack of enthusiasm from history majors about some of the department's faculty and their interaction with students, a factor important to him. To top it off, the tennis coach hadn't been encouraging about his making the team. Jeff was going home with some hard questions and a need to reflect on whether Burgess was a good match for him.

Emma, on the other hand, was excited by what she had found. She didn't much care for a zealous fraternity and sorority system, and Burgess's approach struck just the right note for her. Liberal arts generally, and psychology, English, and science specifically, received excellent reports from students. She especially liked the balance between studies and social activities, and she particularly enjoyed the prospect of being challenged by smart, lively classmates. She had met people engaged in many activities similar to her own interests, and the campus seemed enhanced by the large variety of students coming from all parts of the country. Summing it up, Emma felt good vibes — Burgess had a spirit and ambience that jibed with her desires.

Both Emma and Jeff had done a good job in their investigations. Each had come up with discoveries that filled in the picture of the college, and now each could reach a decision about whether Burgess was a suitable fit.

Getting to the Heart of a College

You won't learn everything about a complex community in a few hours or even an overnight, but you can explore all the areas that interest and concern you. Going armed with knowledge about yourself and the college is the basic preparation for the visit, while curiosity and questions are the order of the day when you're on campus.

When you return home, you can sort out your observations and make your analysis of the college's character, its strengths and its weaknesses. Having gone about the campus visit and interview in an organized, systematic fashion, you will be better qualified to judge whether the college and you make a good match. You will know the real college, and the college will know the real you.

For Parents

Beyond the excitement and anticipation, finding the colleges that best match each student is time intensive and challenging. Some students will need more help than others, and many students will turn to their parents to assist them. This often puts parents in the difficult position of wondering how much help is too much, but always with a nagging worry about how little help is too little.

An important aspect of your family's exploration is the quality of the college. The lists of "best colleges" touted by the magazines do not introduce you and your child to what constitutes a truly good college education. Do not be overly swayed by the prestige of a college that would be a bad fit for your child, nor by the low cost of a school that would not properly prepare your child for life after college. The books listed at the end of this Afterword are excellent sources of information, as are the books and websites listed in Chapter 2.

Some students need to know that the academic department they are interested in is tops; others need to know that the college will provide them with a career; some want classmates they'll have as lifelong friends; still others believe that the town or city in which a campus is located is the most important part of their college experience; and others find that it is the theater or sports opportunities that will mark their college years. Every college varies in each of these dimensions, and students will react differently to what they see and when they see it. The fifth academic quad or climbing wall or black box theater will not seem so special as the first one they see. But over time, throughout the process, each student will get a sense of what he or she thinks is important, and it is essential that parents foster this discovery.

You know your sons and daughters best, and you know how you can help them make good decisions about college. That is true even if you haven't gone to college yourself.

What Parents Need to Know

Parents and the Application Process

Parents of high school students are pulled in all directions these days. You are told not to get too involved in your child's college application process, but also that it takes a family to do it right; you are told to make sure that no mistakes are made in applying to colleges, but not to hover and nag; and you are told to get your financial affairs in order to maximize the chances for financial aid, but to let your child search for scholarships. Obviously, the walk through this minefield is a very tricky one.

Here are some things you can do during the application process:

- Be well informed

- Discuss financial or geographic limitations early on

- Look into financial aid and EFC (Expected Family Contribution)

- Help, or get help, to form a balanced list of colleges

- Pay test and application fees

- Go on college visits, if appropriate

- Brainstorm college essay topics, but *leave the essay writing to your child*

- Supply clerical assistance when necessary

- Proofread, or have another adult proofread, the applications

- Help when asked, but don't take control

- And above all, be supportive, encouraging and reassuring

Be ready to help when asked, but let your child take the lead. Instead of trying to talk all the time about colleges, consider setting aside a half hour each week to check in on your child's thoughts and progress. Perhaps you might want to point out sections of this book that you think your child will find useful or helpful.

Remember that all through the college selection process, your son or daughter is making sound and discerning decisions that will guarantee a good fit and will also help him or her achieve a strong measure of levelheaded independence. Your wise counsel, comfort and supportive assistance can be invaluable contributions.

Parents and Campus Visits

Whenever feasible, it is best that your child arrange the timing of the campus visit with an email or a phone call to the admission office. If it isn't possible for your child to make these calls during business hours, then you can step in and make the arrangements, making sure that the tour, information session and interview fit into your family's schedule. Your child should confirm the arrangements with an email to the appropriate admission person.

If you join your child on campus visits, you will have the opportunity to make direct contact with the financial aid officer, the admission staff member and college students. You may hear things that your child missed or hear things through the ear of experience that might shine a different light on what was spoken or unspoken.

On the tour and in the information session, we hope that your child will be adequately prepared, especially after reading this book, to ask questions of the guide and presenters. You may find that the tours and information sessions are often dominated by parents asking questions. Nevertheless, the look on the assembled students' faces will make it clear that although the parents' questions may be useful, the students will nonetheless be mortified. A cardinal rule to follow on a campus visit with your child is, "Don't Embarrass."

Colleges have changed the way they work with parents. Many colleges overcome the problem of parents dominating the question periods and students wanting their parents to be quiet by offering separate programs for parents. If the college has this type of program, you should feel free to ask questions, especially the tough ones that might be avoided when your child is present. Some colleges offer parents special sessions on financial aid or a Q&A with the admission staff; others set up a classroom with a professor answering parent questions; still others have meal tickets and package deals at hotels. Some may even have online chat groups for parents. The essential fact is that the campus visit and the college interview process are designed for the student to learn more about the campus and the college to learn more about the student; parents should be in the background.

Parents and Interviews

The interview with the admission staff is for your child alone. The admission person wants to have a conversation with your child to find out more about him or her without your being there. Often, after the interview, the admission counselor will meet with you and may ask if you have any questions, in which case it is appropriate to say something. It is best to keep your remarks benign and not take over. After your visit, and after your child writes or emails a thank-you note, it is rare for a parent to get involved, and it is not recommended. Admission counselors want to be in touch with the applicant, not the applicant's parents. If you have a question, discuss it with your child and see if he or she wants to email the counselor.

Always keep in mind that it is the student who is going to enroll in college, not you, the parent.

Questions of Interest to Parents

There are special issues about colleges that you will find helpful to know about and should be part of your input into the quest. Moreover, your knowledge of particular aspects of the college can constructively strengthen the process.

Some of the areas that follow may be more relevant to you than others; some may not be of interest to you at all. It is up to you, the parents, to determine the appropriateness of these topics and what role each plays in the college selection process. Always keep in mind that no college is perfect.

Despite what students may think, parents can and should ask questions, especially as they help their children research their college selections. You should ask appropriate questions on the tours or during the information sessions, but be careful not to monopolize the events. Sometimes the advantages of a program or the disadvantages of a school may only become clear when the questions are explored after your college visit. Here are some questions that you may want to think about and discuss, along with the other questions found throughout this book:

Academics

- Does the school's mission promote the type of education that you think is best for your child? For a specialty? For a career? For specific values?

- Are there required courses or distributive requirements or a core program?

- In addition to the natural exuberance of students, is there vitality about learning and sharing ideas?

- Are freshman courses all lectures or will they have an opportunity to actively participate in class?

- Does your child learn best through the type of courses that are generally offered?

- Is collaborative and/or group work encouraged?

- In what fields are there research opportunities for undergraduates?

- Are there opportunities for internships?

- Are study or trips abroad encouraged? What percentage of students participate?

- Is a senior thesis or capstone experience required?

- What is the freshman retention rate? Are there any special problems?

- What percentage of students graduate in four years? Why do some students need more time?

- What percentage of students go on to graduate school? What graduate schools do they typically attend?

- Is the college enhancing the role of technology in the curriculum?

- Does the college use consortiums to supplement campus courses?

- If a course is not offered, does the college have online options?

Faculty

- Are required undergraduate courses taught by full-time faculty?

- Have there been recent cutbacks in faculty or departments? What about future plans?

- Is there support for development of new courses or new teaching skills?

- What is the reputation of professors in your child's proposed major?

- Do professors encourage students to assist in research? In what areas?

- Is there informal interaction between professor and student?

- Do individual professors know students by their first names?

Campus Life

- Is there a good balance of academic, social, cultural and recreational opportunities?

- Is diversity respected? Does the enrollment reflect the national composition?

- Are there any special issues on campus that indicate problems?

- Is an international point of view promoted?

- Is community service encouraged? What percentage of students are engaged in volunteer work? What range of activities is covered?

- How are cultural events integrated into campus activities?

Safety and Health

- What is the campus security system? Are there complaints?

- Is there good nighttime lighting?

- What provisions are there for shuttle service or security escorts?

- How many and what kinds of crime occurred on campus last year? (Statistics are available through http://ope.ed.gov/security.)

- Has the college had any recent campus-wide emergency? When? What happened? What has changed since then? Is there an emergency communications plan?

- Have there been any hate crimes? When? What happened? What was the result?

- How can students call for help?

- Is there ongoing education about date rape, binge drinking and substance abuse?

- Will you be notified if your child commits a serious infraction of the rules, e.g., alcohol violation, drug abuse, cheating or plagiarism, or sexual harassment?

- What specific health services does the college provide?

- Are there on-campus and outreach mental health services?

- Is there access to specialists? How is that billed?

- Is counseling readily available?

- What is covered by insurance?

- How close is the nearest hospital?

Financial Issues

- What is the financial health of the college?

- Is the college cutting out certain departments or courses?

- Is any program in jeopardy for financial reasons?

- Are class sizes increasing?

- Is enrollment increasing?

- How much has the endowment grown in the last seven years?

- Have there been any recent fund-raising campaigns? Did the college reach its goal? What percentage of alumni contributed? Who else contributed?

- Has the college recently received any special gifts? For what purpose?

- How much of a tuition hike is anticipated? Is tuition being capped in any way?

- Are the mandatory fees increasing?

- How does the library budget compare with those of other college departments — athletics, for example?

- What arrangements are made for tech support? Are there extra fees?

- Does financial aid stay the same for the four years? Are there restrictions?

- Are merit scholarships awarded? If one is awarded, will it continue for four years?

- Are there plans for future expansion?

Special Services

- Who will be your child's freshman advisor? Does the advisor change with the declaration of a major?

- What support services are there for students who need help to keep up?

- Does the college have its own study abroad programs or does it link with other colleges?

- What services does the career center offer? Does it help with internships? Jobs?

- Does the school sponsor GRE, MCAT and LSAT prep courses for grad school?

- Whom should parents contact if they have concerns? (For parents of student with special needs, see Chapter 7.)

You may follow up on any of these issues. The college process should be interactive and allow for questions that you and your child can share to air your concerns.

After Admission

Colleges want accepted students to enroll at their college, and therefore many have special programs for accepted students, and parents are often encouraged to join in. Colleges want to engage and interest parents in the college community by holding informative meetings, talks, walks, brunches and lunches that open up the campus scene, but still separate students from parents. They want students to have their own distinct experiences at these campus events. But they want both student and parents to find their particular school irresistible, and so these activities, both for students and parents, are filled with interesting and exciting aspects of campus life.

If your child will be living away from home, foster independence and good decision making by helping your child learn how to work out problems, do laundry, open a bank account, write checks or bank online. Talk about the uses and abuses of credit and debit cards. If you wish, you can discuss particular worries you have about your child living away, remembering that you won't have as much direct contact as both of you are used to.

Some parents may particularly value family closeness and want their student near home or even living at home and making the daily commute to school. There are good reasons to take this direction, but many students will flourish by living on their own. If this is a concern, take advantage of guidance sessions at your child's high school to better understand the advantages of a residential college.

After Enrollment

In bygone days, college was viewed as an ivory tower, far removed from the world and its woes. Nowadays, civilization and all its discontents have encroached on that idyllic scene. Problems that exist on the outside are part of campus life. And not all of that is bad: students are now more actively engaged in the community outside the campus as they deal with environmental concerns or tutoring of neighborhood school children. Some students become involved with the working conditions of campus support staff; others are engaged in national or local politics.

Life's temptations — alcohol, drugs, safe and unsafe sex and cheating — are also present on campus. Your son or daughter will most likely be facing these issues, and, in some cases, may already have faced them in high school. How the individual student deals with these matters is a part of growing up. As a parent, you will not have a daily awareness of your child's activities, but you can learn beforehand how these issues are handled on each campus.

As part of keeping parents informed, colleges, as a follow-up after enrollment, generally provide online newsletters to make parents aware of activities and events, and also to solicit their support beyond tuition dollars. When freshman students move in and attend orientation sessions, there may be parallel programs for parents. In addition, almost all colleges hold a

Parents' Weekend in the fall semester with talks by the president, meetings with faculty and many social events for parents only. Some schools have a handbook for parents and a particular person to contact if you have a concern or a question to ask. Still others have picnics, barbecues and homecoming invitations.

All these activities are designed to keep you in touch with the campus — but at arm's length. It is so easy nowadays to reach out by cell phone, texting, email, Facebook and the like, and administrators know that it is important for parents to stay in touch with their children. But they also know that some of the greatest learning comes when students ponder questions and make their own mistakes. Colleges, just like parents, want students to gain independence and make their own decisions. They hope that by providing lots of information and special days on campus, parents will stand back and not be too involved in their children's day-to-day actions.

The journey to finding those colleges that best match your child's needs, wishes and hopes can be a meaningful one for the whole family. We hope that this book will help you navigate this course with better preparation and greater knowledge of two essentials of the process, the campus visit and the college interview.

Books for Parents

Besides the resources listed in Chapter 2, the following books are recommended particularly for parents:

- *First in the Family: Your College Years: Advice About College from First-Generation Students*. Kathleen Cushman. Providence, RI: Next Generation Press, 2006.

- *The iConnected Parent*. Barbara Hofer and Abigail Sullivan Moore. Glencoe, IL: Free Press, 2010.

- *Less Stress, More Success*. Marilee Jones and Kenneth R. Ginsburg. Elk Grove Village, IL: American Academy of Pediatrics, 2006.

- *Letting Go*. Karen Levin Coburn and Madge Laurence Treeger. New York: HarperCollins, 5th edition, 2009.

- *Parents' Guide to College Life*. Robin Raskin. New York: Random House, 2006.

- *Smart Parents Guide to College*. Ernest L. Boyer and Paul Boyer. Princeton, NJ: Peterson's. 1996.

Notes on Colleges Visited

College _____

Date Visited _____

Notes _____

_____

_____

_____

_____

_____

_____

_____

_____

_____

_____

_____

_____

_____

_____

_____

_____

_____

_____

_____

_____

_____

_____

Notes on Colleges Visited

College _____

Date Visited _____

Notes _____

_____

_____

_____

_____

_____

_____

_____

_____

_____

_____

_____

_____

_____

_____

_____

_____

_____

_____

_____

_____

_____